A Month with JESUS

A Month with JESUS

31 DAYS

WITH A SURPRISING SAVIOR

Gary Holloway

LEAFWOOD PUBLISHERS

To Julia Keith, who shows Jesus to all around her

A MONTH WITH JESUS

31 Days with a Surprising Savior

LEAFWOOD
PUBLISHERS

ISBN 978-0-89112-361-3

Printed in the United States of America

Cover design by Rick Gibson
Interior text design by Sandy Armstrong

Leafwood Publishers
1626 Campus Court
Abilene, Texas 79601
1-877-816-4455 toll free

For current information about all Leafwood titles, visit our Web site:
www.leafwoodpublishers.com

12 13 14 15 16 17 / 7 6 5 4 3 2 1

Contents

Introduction

We know our Bibles. If there is one thing that has marked conservative Christians, it's our knowledge of the Bible. We know it backwards and forwards. We can tell the stories and quote the verses. No sermon or Bible lesson can catch us off guard, because we know the Book.

Or do we? Could it be that our own familiarity with the Bible blinds us to the impact it must have had on its original readers?

William Willimon, a Methodist minister, tells how one Sunday his six-year-old son informed him, "I'm not going to Sunday School today." Of course, he had to go anyway, but Willimon was curious about his reluctance.

"Why don't you want to go?"

"Because they never do anything new there," he replied. "It's always, 'Jesus, Jesus, Jesus.'"

This book promises nothing new, only the old "Jesus, Jesus, Jesus." But do we know the real Jesus? "Of course, we do," you reply. We know him backward and forward. We know every story about him. Birth stories, the Sermon on the Mount, miracles, parables, betrayal, arrest, crucifixion, resurrection, we know them all by heart.

Or do we?

Is it really Jesus we know or just our picture of Jesus that we've substituted for the real thing? When we think of Jesus, we feel comfortable. He's the Jesus who loves us, who makes us feel warm inside. When his contemporaries saw the real Jesus they had quite a different reaction: they were shocked, amazed, and surprised. Jesus never did what they expected him to do. They couldn't predict or control him, they could only stare open-mouthed in astonishment.

Maybe the same old thing of "Jesus, Jesus, Jesus" in our churches has blinded us to who he really was and really is. Perhaps our own walk with him is not what it should be because we feel too comfortable with him, or at least of our picture of him. This is an invitation to spend a month with the biblical Jesus, the one who surprised his contemporaries. By looking at him through their eyes, maybe we too can be surprised. Surprised enough to shake us out of our old habits. Surprised enough to understand him as never before. Surprised enough to follow. Surprised enough that this familiar story, the greatest story of all, is no longer "the same old thing."

So, I invite you into this strange world of the miracles of Jesus. A world where the blind are healed, the lame walk, the demon-possessed are freed, where people drink miraculous wine, walk on water, and even rise from the dead. By entering this world we come to see that it is our world. That the power that worked through Jesus still works in our lives through faith. That God still heals the sick, comforts the grieving, defeats the devil, and rules the winds and waves.

DAY 1

So You Think You Know Jesus?

Mark 6:1-6; Matthew 16:13-28; Luke 19:1-9

Who's the Bible character you know best?

Surely, it's Jesus.

We all know Jesus. We sing about his birth, study his teachings, marvel at his miracles, thrill at his resurrection.

Church folks especially know Jesus. We've heard countless sermons and Bible lessons on him. We study his life in small groups and in personal Bible study. If there's one character in the Bible we know, it's Jesus.

Or do we? Do we really know Jesus? Even if we're Christians and have studied him all our lives, is it possible we can miss his full significance?

There were those in his own day who were sure they knew him. They grew up with him. They followed him. He called them disciples. Yet, when it really came down to it, they didn't know who he was. They thought they did, but he always had a way of surprising them. Just when they thought they had a handle on who this Jesus was, he'd do something that turned their world upside down. "Who is this?" they asked.

Could the same thing happen to us?

The Hometown Folks (Mark 6:1-6)

"Isn't this the carpenter?" Mark 6:3a

If there was anyone who knew Jesus, you'd think it would be the people he grew up with. They played games with him as a kid, "hide-and-go-seek" and "tag." They saw him struggle with them to learn Hebrew in the synagogue school. They swapped stories with his dad in the carpenter's shop. They knew his mom and his brothers and sisters.

They also knew that he'd become a traveling preacher. They'd heard stories about him that were hard to believe. Some said he was the best teacher they'd ever heard. Some said he had healed lepers, cast out demons, and even raised a little girl from the dead.

Now he was coming home to Nazareth. Speaking in their synagogue. Local boy makes good.

They couldn't wait to hear him.

They weren't disappointed.

He taught with a wisdom they'd never heard before. He did amazing things they'd never seen before.

How do the hometown folks react? With pride? "He's one of us, a local boy. I knew him when." With faith? With obedience? Do they fall at his feet and worship him as God in the flesh?

No. They are offended.

"Who does he think he is?" they asked.

"He's just a carpenter."

"He fixed my roof."

"He built my porch."

"Why, that's just Jimmy's brother; I know his family. Where does he get off claiming to be someone special?"

Familiarity breeds contempt. So it was with Jesus' hometown folks. As the NIV says, "And they took offense at him."

Offended by Jesus. It's an interesting concept. His teaching and wisdom are so amazing, his claims to power and to fellowship with God are so outrageous, that they offend the sensibilities of those who thought they knew him best. Have you ever been offended by Jesus?

The Greek word for offended here is *skandalizo,* from which we get the word "scandalized." Jesus' words and actions were a scandal, an embarrassment to his hometown. Earlier in Mark we are told that Jesus' own family came "to take charge of him, for they said, 'He is out of his mind'" (Mark 3:21). One can hear his brothers and sisters shaking their heads and saying, "That crazy Jesus. What does he think he's doing? Who does he think he is?"

The answer, of course, is that he thought he was God. What if your brother met strangers on the street and said, "Hello, I'm Jesus Christ?" Wouldn't you think he's crazy? Wouldn't you try (for his own good) to get him some professional help. We have places for people who claim to be God. We call those places "mental hospitals." If Jesus was not really the Son of God, then he was crazy or worse.

Jesus claimed to be the Son of God. His family and friends in Nazareth thought him crazy and were embarrassed by him. As other translations put it, "they stumbled because of him." His actions "tripped them up." My students still use this phrase for a tough question on an exam. "That one tripped me up." The Nazarenes fail to answer correctly the most important question of all: "Who is Jesus?" The ones who should have known him best, didn't know him at all.

Jesus marveled at their unbelief. "And he was amazed at their lack of faith" (Mark 6:6). We too are amazed. How could they be so blind? But there is a warning here. Might it be that we who know Jesus best (or think we do), really don't know him at all?

The Answer Man (Matthew 16:13-28)

"But what about you?' he asked. 'Who do you say I am?'" Matthew 16:15

But of course we know Jesus better than his hometown folks. They didn't believe in Jesus. We do. We confess him as Lord and Christ. They thought he was just a carpenter. We know better. We know he is the Son of God.

There was another who knew who Jesus was. He was "the answer man" among Jesus' disciples. Since "disciple" means "student," you might even call this man the smartest boy in class. When the other students of Jesus were unsure and silent about who Jesus was and what he was doing, this man always came up with the answer. Sometimes he was even right.

We call him Peter.

After spending a great deal of time in class with Jesus, the disciples are given a test.

Question one: "Who do people say the Son of Man is?" (Matthew 16:13).

All the disciples get this one right. From different corners of the classroom come shouted answers. "John the Baptist." "Elijah." "Jeremiah." "One of the prophets."

Question two (the hard one): "Who do you say I am?"

Silence. No one answers for a while. It's the most important question ever asked and still the disciples hesitate.

Until Peter jumps in. "You are the Christ, the Son of the living God."

"You're right!" Jesus says. Or (even better) he actually says, "Blessed are you, Simon, son of Jonah."

Peter knows who Jesus is. He gets the answer right just as we get it right. How does he know who Jesus is? Not because he's really the best student. Not because he'd studied more, or thought more, or been with Jesus more. No. He gets the answer right because he "cheated." He got the answer from someone else. From God himself. "This was not revealed to you by man, but by my Father in heaven" (Matthew 16:17).

God reveals to Peter that Jesus is the Christ. Peter knew, as surely as we know, that Jesus was the Son of God. He knew it. He confessed it. That settled it.

But he really didn't understand.

Immediately after Peter's confession, Jesus begins to explain to the disciples that he must go to Jerusalem, suffer under the authorities, be killed, and be raised to life.

Peter knows that can't be true. The Messiah was to reign over Israel in righteousness. If Jesus is killed by the authorities, then his mission is a complete failure. Peter and the other disciples didn't sign on with Jesus because they thought he would fail. They knew that a dead man cannot be the Messiah. Peter had just confessed Jesus as Messiah, but now Jesus is talking about suffering and shame and failure.

Jesus must be confused.

So Peter does the loving thing. He takes Jesus aside quietly and tries to show him the error of his ways.

Then Jesus turns the tables: "Get behind me, Satan!" he says to Peter. "You are a stumbling block to me; you do not have in mind the things of God, but the things of men" (Matthew 16:23). Peter has gone from being called "blessed," to being called "Satan." The people of Nazareth were tripped up on the question of Jesus' identity. Here, Peter tries to trip up Jesus (Greek, *skandalon*). Peter unintentionally tempts Jesus as Satan had tempted him in the wilderness. He offers him the kingdoms of the world without suffering. He offers the crown before the cross. A triumphant, reigning Messiah is the only kind that Peter can imagine.

We are amazed at Peter. How can he confess Jesus as Messiah and Son of God and then turn around and rebuke Jesus? What audacity, to think he knows better than the Lord. How blind can Peter be?

Are we any better? "Sure we are," you say. "We know that Jesus had to suffer. We know he came to die for us. We know he was raised from the dead."

But do we know any better than Peter what it means to die with him? That's what Jesus calls Peter and us to do: "If anyone would come after me, he must deny himself and take up his cross and follow me" (Matthew 16:24).

The Chief of the Cheats (Luke 19:1-9)

"He wanted to see who Jesus was. . . ." Luke 19:3a

Have I convinced you yet? Have I convinced you that no matter how well we think we know Jesus, in some ways we don't know him at all?

Those who should have known him best, his hometown folks, didn't know him at all. They didn't want to. The disciple who should have known him best, who confesses him as Christ, doesn't understand what that means.

But there is one who is the least likely candidate to know him. Least likely because he is a notorious sinner. A tax collector.

I know we all get upset with the IRS. We think they take too much money from us, make their forms unnecessarily complicated, and sometimes abuse their authority.

The IRS is nothing compared to first-century tax collectors. They basically made up their own tax rates based on how much they thought they could get out of people. And they taxed you every way they could. There were taxes on crops, houses, and slaves. There were custom taxes on shipped goods, tolls on roads, and even a poll tax.

Worst of all, the tax collectors worked for the Romans. They were traitors to God's people. They took the hard-earned money of the poor of Israel and sent it to support a pagan conqueror. By associating with their Gentile overlords, the tax collectors became ceremonially unclean.

In short, they were slimy, treacherous cheats.

And Zacchaeus was their chief.

So, one day Jesus comes to Jericho. The townspeople wonder, "Where will he go to eat? Whose house will this great rabbi grace? Will he choose the mayor? A righteous keeper of the law? A godly widow?"

None of the above. He goes to eat with Zacchaeus. The chief tax collector. The head cheat. The worst of sinners. The townspeople are amazed. They mutter, "He has gone to be the guest of a sinner."

Not only does Jesus eat with Zacchaeus, he even tells him, "Today salvation has come to this house."

What had Zacchaeus done to deserve all this? Was he better than people gave him credit for? No, he was all they said and more. So what had he done to get Jesus to his house?

One thing. One thing only. "He wanted to see who Jesus was" (Luke 19:3). That's all. He wanted to see who Jesus was. He wanted it so badly that he climbed a tree. He wanted it so badly he gave half his goods to the poor. He wanted it so badly he paid back four-fold those whom he had cheated.

What does it take to know Jesus? You have to want to. Badly. More than you want anything or anyone.

Only then can we know him.

After proclaiming salvation had come to Zacchaeus's house, Jesus says, "For the Son of Man came to seek and to save what was lost" (Luke 19:10). He comes to those who do not know him, but he comes only where he is wanted.

So you think you know Jesus?
Think again.
Do you want to know Jesus?
That's the question.

DAY 2

A Word for the Day

John 1:1-14

"Talk is cheap." "They're only words." "Don't tell me, show me."

We are constantly bombarded by words. On television, radio, billboards, newspapers, online, through the phone. Lectures, meetings, sermons, conversations. Too many words! No wonder we express ourselves in the phrases above. Overwhelmed with talk we find words empty and shallow.

But think of the power of great words in history: Abraham Lincoln's Gettysburg Address rallies a nation in time of war; Martin Luther King's "I Have a Dream" speech leads to the liberation of a people. Words do have power.

God Speaks

Words from God particularly have power. His words are never empty. They do something!

God speaks. Light, earth, seas, plants, animals all spring into existence. God talks with Adam and Eve in the garden. God warns Noah. He calls Abraham. He speaks to Moses from the burning bush. He thunders his promises from Mount Sinai. He whispers to Elijah. He says things through the prophets.

God speaks. What good news that is! God did not leave us alone surrounded by a myriad of competing voices all vying for our attention. He loved us enough to speak. To guide. To instruct. The Old Testament is not a book of rules, but a series of gentle instructions from a loving Father to his beloved children.

God's Word in Flesh

But God did more than speak words. He is the Word.

> In the beginning was the Word, and the Word was with God, and the Word was God. He was with God in the beginning.
>
> Through him all things were made; without him nothing was made that has been made. In him was life, and that life was the light of men. The light shines in the darkness, but the darkness has not understood it.
>
> The Word became flesh and made his dwelling among us. We have seen his glory, the glory of the One and Only, who came from the Father, full of grace and truth. John 1:1-5, 14

Jesus is the Word. Many of us even know the original Greek word here—*logos. Logos* was a rich word, a loaded term in the ancient world. It can mean word, thought, speech, or principle. Ancient philosophers used it to refer to a rational principle behind all human action. What is important here is not the background of the word, but the way John describes this *logos.*

This Word is God. Not just divine. Not simply like God. He is God. Whatever we mean by "God" must include this Word named Jesus. This is why Christians believe in the Trinity. Our view of Jesus forces us to. We believe God is one, but not simply one. We believe in God the Father who made heaven and earth but we also believe Jesus is God. The Spirit, too. Yet we do not believe in three Gods, but in one. The word is God. Thus at the heart of the mystery of God we find relationship and community.

This Word created the world. Not just part of the world, but everything that was created. This Word is not empty talk but is powerful enough to call all things into existence.

This Word is light. "Let there be light." He is more than the light that shines each day. He is the light that shines in every human heart. Darkness fights the light but cannot overcome it.

This Word became flesh. How can that be? The eternal become temporal? Immortality become mortal? Yes. That is the strange mystery we believe, that God the Word actually became human. He did not pretend to be one of us. He did not become like us in some ways. He is one of us. In the flesh he knows hunger, pain, rejection, and death. He becomes one of us so he might make us like him.

What a powerful Word! So powerful that he can become weak. Weak for us. So weak that through him we are empowered to be the children of God.

God's Word Written

The word of God. When the Gospel of John uses the phrase, it obviously refers to Jesus. But when most Christians today speak of the word of God, we mean something else. We mean the Bible.

The Bible is the word of God. God revealed himself to many through the centuries. Some, through the power of God and inspiration of the Holy Spirit, wrote of those experiences of God speaking. We call their writings Scripture. God's word written.

So what is the word of God? Is it Jesus or the Bible? The answer is, "Yes."

But we must not equate the two. There is a relationship between Jesus and the Scriptures. The Bible is not the ultimate word of God. Jesus is. The Scriptures point to Jesus as God's best and final word. Indeed, one can be a great Bible scholar and still miss Jesus, the true Word of God.

Jesus himself confronts some who had done that very thing:

> And the Father who sent me has himself testified concerning me. You have never heard his voice nor seen his form, nor does his word dwell in you, for you do not believe the one he sent. You diligently study the Scriptures because you think that by them you possess eternal life. These are the Scriptures that testify about me, yet you refuse to come to me to have life. John 5:37-40

Jesus speaks to those who knew their Bibles. They firmly believed in the inspiration and authority of Scripture. They considered themselves experts in the Bible. They could argue and debate over its meaning. They were greatly offended if anyone implied they did not know or did not follow their Bibles.

Yet somehow they missed the very point of the Bible. They missed Jesus.

Could such a thing happen today? Could it happen to us? Many of us pride ourselves in being Bible Christians. We look down on those who (in our way of thinking) lessen its authority or pervert its teaching. We can quote chapter and verse. We can argue over the meaning of words.

But do we miss Jesus? I have known those who are full of Bible knowledge but who are cranky, mean, and narrow. More than know them, I have been one of them. The Bible itself warns against "unhealthy interest in controversies and quarrels about words that result in envy, strife, malicious talk, evil suspicions and constant friction" (1Timothy 6:4). We can be right on the Bible and wrong on Jesus. Wrong because we do not let his words and his Spirit control our lives.

God did not leave us alone without a word from him. He spoke at many times and in many ways. But now he has given us his final and best word. The Word made flesh. Jesus. No better word is coming, so we better listen to this one!

DAY 3

Treasures of the Heart

Luke 1-2

Every family has its stories of the funny things children say and do. They make for great entertainment and are also good for embarrassing the child once he becomes a teenager. Our nephew, Adam, is now in college, but when he was three he was just at the age where he did at least one cute thing a day. He enjoyed making up his own words. "Pinkawink," he'd say, or "tant-tant." Then he'd cut his eyes toward whoever was listening and grin. He knew these were not real words, but they were especially his.

Like most children (and adults), he was most funny when he wasn't trying to be. When he really wanted you to do something, and you didn't want to do it, he'd say, "No, honey, do this." Somewhere he's learned that "honey" takes the sting out of "no." He was even funny when he was bad. Once he couldn't find the toy he was looking for in his bedroom, so he said, "Darn, darn." My wife overheard him and asked, "Adam, did you say a bad word." A shocked look came over his face and he answered sheepishly and with tears, "Aunt Deb, I think I did say a bad word."

All families have such stories. All children say and do the most surprising things. What sometimes surprises parents the most is what others say about their little darlings. "I just couldn't keep Sandy from talking today in Sunday school," the teacher says. That's quite a shock since she won't speak five words at home. "Mark was a perfect gentleman when he stayed with us overnight." So says the neighbor; but you wonder, "Our Mark?"

We laugh at our children. We wonder at what others say about them. Most of all, we try to imagine what life has in store for them. Will they find their place in the world? Will they be happy? Can we spare them from much of the sorrow that life throws at us all? Along with our treasured memories of their childhood, these are the questions that haunt us most.

Mary had strange stories to tell about her son, Jesus. Stories of what he did. Stories of what others said about him. In faith, she had faced the great surprise from Gabriel, "The Holy Spirit will come upon you and you will bear a son." Yet that was just the first of many surprises. There was more to come. More than she could imagine. More than she could understand. Below are four stories Mary could have told. Stories of this strange son who surprised and baffled her. Treasured memories.

The Unexpected Baby

"How can this be?" 1:34b (NRSV)

No one expected this baby. Certainly not Mary. She was an ordinary young woman expecting an ordinary life. She would marry Joseph the carpenter, have his children, and live quietly in her hometown of Nazareth.

Or so she thought. Until the day an angel appeared to her, and no ordinary angel but Gabriel himself. "Greetings, The Lord is very pleased with you," he said.

Mary was floored, startled by the angel and his strange greeting. But she hadn't heard nothing yet.

"You're going to have a baby and you'll name him Jesus."

Although a young, uneducated girl, she knew where babies came from. She knew she could not be pregnant, since she was a virgin. Yet somehow a child was growing inside her.

In shock, she still replied in faith, "So be it."

Who expected this baby? Certainly not Joseph. What a shock to learn that his young fiancée was pregnant! They had not slept together. He trusted her completely. He knew her heart, her purity, her honesty. So when she told him she was carrying a child, he didn't know what to think. "Who is the father?" he asked. She answered, "No one, at least no man."

And somehow he believed her.

And yet he didn't. Surely no one else would. He could not stand to see her punished for what she obviously had done, yet he could not marry her. A quiet divorce was the only way out.

Joseph certainly did not expect the explanation he ultimately received. An angel appeared to Joseph, frightening him with his presence and bewildering him with his words. "This child is of the Holy Spirit." "Do not be afraid."

No one expected the baby to be born here. Not in Bethlehem.

The child was supposed to be born in Nazareth, where Mary could be at home with her mother. But the Romans had ordered a census, so off to Bethlehem they must go. Bethlehem, the town of their ancestors, though they had never been there and did not know a soul.

"Where will we stay?" Mary asked. "We have no family there."

"Surely you've heard of inns, woman." Joseph testily replied, tired from the long journey and the constant worry over Mary and the coming child.

But there was no room at the inn. So the child was born in a stable, probably one hewn from the rocks. Born in a cave. Laid in a manger. Ox and donkey were his midwives. Calves and colts his nursery mates.

This was the Son of God? The King of the Jews? Indeed. God had surprised mankind as a child. Born to a common couple. Born in a stable. Born to rule the world.

Born to surprise.

Just Another Night

". . . and they were terrified." Luke 2:9b

Avram was a shepherd. His father was a shepherd as was his father before him.

Avram was bored, and if there's one thing shepherds know, its boredom. This night promised to be like so many nights before it. Nothing ever happened and there was nothing to do. Even his fellow shepherds could not relieve Avram's boredom, for he knew them too well. Night after night they had the same conversations about politics and women and the same arguments over who was the strongest and who was the brightest.

Bored. Utterly bored.

Suddenly, he was bored no longer. For a bright light, brighter than mid-day shone around them, and a glorious being descended, a messenger from God. Avram's boredom turned to terror.

But the angel said, "Don't be afraid; I bring good news. The Messiah is born in Bethlehem. Here's how you'll recognize him: he's a baby, lying in loose cloths in a manger."

Then with a tremendous roar it seemed the stars themselves began to sing. An army of angels descended, singing praises to God.

It was over as suddenly as it had begun. "Did you see that?" the shepherds asked each other, for none was sure if it was real, or a vision, or if he had simply lost his wits. But all had seen it. Angels had appeared, not to rabbis or kings or men of wealth, but to common working men.

"We've got to go see this baby," said Avram, and all agreed. So they left their flocks ("After all," one said, "if God can send an army of angels, he can surely watch our sheep") and came to Bethlehem and found the child, lying in the manger and praised God for him.

Why did God send angels to shepherds? Informing wise men, yes, that we can understand, but common shepherds? Among the Jews shepherds were generally regarded as ignorant and dishonest outlaws. Why them?

Because they were precisely the people this child came to save. Not the rich and powerful. Not kings and princes. Not the well, but the sick. Common people. Plain folks. And when these plain shepherds heard the news, they knew how to respond. They hurry, they see, they praise.

Mary was surprised by these shepherds. She didn't quite understand, but "treasured up all these things and pondered them in her heart" (Luke 2:19). We may not fully understand them either. We live far away from these shepherds, far away in time, in space, and in culture. But though we live in a different world, one they could hardly imagine, we still seek the same child they seek. And in some ways, we meet him in the same way. For the good news comes to us in the midst of our boring tasks, when we least expect it. Sometimes it hits us with such force that, like them, we quake in terror: The Savior of the world is born.

The question is: Do we have the same simple trusting faith they had? The faith to leave behind our jobs, our hopes, our dreams, all the "flocks" that bind us and to go to kneel before that Child? For the angel call is to us, as well as to them, good news of great joy to all people.

Great Expectations

"And the child's father and mother were amazed at what was being said about him." Luke 2:33 (NRSV)

The old guy looked pretty scary. Mary and Joseph weren't sure they wanted him to hold their new baby. Even if this was the temple, this old man Simeon looked pretty strange. They were cautious about entrusting their child to him.

After all, they had big plans for this new son of theirs named Jesus. For months, Joseph had anticipated fatherhood. No doubt the boy would be a big help to him in his business. Joseph and Son, Carpenters. It had a nice ring to it. After the strangeness of the child's conception and the wild trip to Bethlehem, Mary and Joseph were looking forward to returning home to Nazareth. All they needed to do was make this quick trip to Jerusalem for the purification sacrifice. Then back to home and a normal life.

But now in the temple, this old guy Simeon wanted to hold the child. "Go ahead," Joseph told Mary, "let him hold the baby so we can get out of here and head for home."

> So Simeon took the child in his arms and broke out in song:
>
> "Sovereign Lord, as you have promised,
> you now dismiss your servant in peace.
> For my eyes have seen your salvation,
> which you have prepared in the sight of all people.
> a light for revelation to the Gentiles
> and for glory to your people Israel." Luke 2:29-32

"What did you say?" cried Joseph.

"I said you are blessed because this child will save Israel, yes and even the world," replied Simeon.

They were shocked by these words.

But that wasn't the end of their strange day in the temple. As they turned to leave an old woman accosted them. "This is the child," she said in a loud voice, "This is the child I have waited on all my life, the one who will redeem Israel." Her loud cries drew a crowd around Mary and Joseph. They were embarrassed and confused by all this attention. Anyone who passed by would be grabbed by the old woman Anna, "Look, look," she said, pointing to the baby, "he is the one!"

Finally they made their escape from the temple. They left convinced the old guy and the aged woman were indeed strange, and they returned to Nazareth and their old, normal life. But twelve years later, there was another surprise.

In My Father's Things

". . . they did not understand what he was saying to them." Luke 2:50

Mary just didn't understand the boy. You would think he'd show more responsibility. Sure, he was only twelve, but there was no excuse for him getting lost like this.

Joseph blamed her and himself. "Why didn't you watch him?" he asked her (and himself). "Where did you last see him?"

"In the city," she replied.

"Perhaps he's with our relatives, "they thought. So they went up and down the caravan, calling "Jesus, Jesus."

But there was no answer.

"Lost your boy, hey Joseph? Mighty irresponsible of you," they teased.

Mary didn't laugh. "We have to go back for him."

And so they did. Re-crossing the miles on foot, each step bringing imagined terrors. "Did the robbers get him?" "Was he kidnapped?" "Is he starving?" "Will some kind soul take him in?"

Finally they were back to the city gates. Jerusalem was such a big place. Where to look?

"Have you seen a little boy? Dark hair, about this tall, with a blue ribbon around the hem of his robe? No? Well, thanks anyway."

Desperate. Frantic. Sick with fear, hunger, and fatigue, they finally try the temple.

And there he was, pretty as you please. Bothering the rabbis. But they really don't look bothered.

"Son, where have you been? Don't you know your dad and I were worried sick?"

"But mom, you knew I'd be in my Father's workshop."

That made no sense to them.

But the boy was found. He came home and was as helpful and respectful as he had always been. He played and learned and grew like other boys.

But he was not like other boys. He was the Savior, the Son of God. Mary was shocked at his actions and words in the temple. Why? How could she be surprised? She knew he was born of a virgin. She could remember angels and shepherds and Simeon and Anna. Why didn't she know he would be in the temple with his Father?

The answer must be that he had been such a normal boy for twelve years. A boy like all boys. Just as we sometimes experience with our own children, Mary needed some outsiders (the teachers in the temple) to show her what her boy was really like.

Mary must have thought often of that day and what the boy possibly could have meant about "his Father's workshop." But she soon forgot. After all, the boy never did anything strange like that again.

At least not until he was about thirty

DAY 4

The Cart before the Horse

Matthew 3:13-17

How can one recognize a street preacher?

The answer's too obvious: because he's on the street. However, that's not the only thing that sets them apart. They dress funny. Some wear clothes that are merely out of style, but others have created special costumes for themselves with large crosses around their necks and homemade robes of black or white.

They also carry Bibles. Some of them have the biggest Bibles I've ever seen, with hand-tooled leather covers full of Christian symbols. I've never seen a street preacher actually read from a Bible, but they do use them effectively as props, waving them in the faces of passers-by to get their attention.

Then there are their eyes. They all have a wild look in their eyes as if they can see what others cannot.

Their message is also distinctive. "Repent," "turn," "change," are staples of their preaching vocabulary. And the message is delivered at the top of their voices, perhaps to drown out the noise of passing traffic but more likely to impress their listeners with the importance of their subject.

If you think I'm making fun, you are mistaken. Street preachers remind me of John the Baptist. I wonder what people thought about him. He didn't preach on the street, but in the desert. He certainly dressed strangely, a camel hair robe and leather belt, the traditional dress of a wilderness prophet (2 Kings 1:8). He even ate strangely—locusts and wild honey. His message was the distinctive prophetic message: "Repent or face the judgment of God."

Whatever people thought, John knew what he was about. He had his calling, his job to do. He was there to prepare the way of the Lord. But even John was to be surprised at the way the Lord made for himself.

Asking the Wrong Person

"I need to be baptized by you. . . ." Matthew 3:14b

It wasn't supposed to happen this way.

Even before his birth, he was destined to be a follower. John was to prepare the way for the Messiah, to smooth over the rough spots, to make an easy path, an open highway for him.

So John went into the wilderness preaching repentance and baptism. Crowds flocked to him and he baptized so many they even nicknamed him, "the Big Dipper," the Baptist. As much as he was admired, he made it clear that his work was all preliminary. He was not the main show, but just the opening act. He couldn't wait to get the spotlight off himself and on to the Messiah. He longed to be the follower he was destined to be.

Then it happened. One day the Messiah came. John was overjoyed. At last he could lay his burden down.

But Messiah Jesus made a strange request. He wanted John to baptize him!

"No way, Lord," John cried. "You've got it all wrong. Like I told the crowd, I'm not even worthy to carry your sandals. How can I baptize you?"

"Let it be," said Jesus.

"But you don't understand, Lord," John persisted. "This baptism is for sinners, it's a baptism for repentance. You're putting the cart before the horse. You don't need to repent; I do. Here, you baptize me, that makes more sense."

"No," said Jesus. "It is right for me to be baptized to fulfill all righteousness."

Finally, John reluctantly consented. He took Jesus, plunged him beneath the water, and brought him back up. Suddenly all heaven broke loose. The Spirit descended and a heavenly voice said, "This is my beloved Son with whom I am well pleased."

From John's perspective, it made no sense. Jesus had no sins to confess, no reason to be baptized. The Messiah was not to come this way. He was to come with power, with the Holy Spirit, and with fire. But this Messiah came in humility. Not baptizing, but being baptized. Not identifying himself as Messiah, but sharing the lot of an ordinary sinner. Perhaps this is one reason why later John will send messengers to ask Jesus, "Are you the one who was to come, or should we expect someone else?" (Matthew 11:2). Jesus didn't come like John expected. He came like a sinner. He came to be baptized.

Yet in this humble act of baptism, Jesus is recognized as the Christ. Recognized by the only one who mattered, by his heavenly Father. Drenched with water, his hair plastered to his skull, he must have looked like all the other penitent sinners. But no. The heavens open, the Spirit comes, the Voice speaks. This is the beloved Son of God.

Where do we see Jesus? Do we see him in power and glory, the great and fiery judge? Yes. But first we see him baptized like the lowliest sinner. John was sure Jesus was Messiah, but he didn't come the way John expected. The star of the show made his entrance quietly, sitting with the audience in the cheap seats.

The beloved Son of God was one of us.

One of Us

"Let it be so now; it is proper for us to do this to fulfill all righteousness."

Matthew 3:15

The story of Jesus' baptism is so familiar that we are not shocked, as John was. But if you think about it, it does make little sense for Jesus to be baptized. John called for repentance. Jesus had nothing to repent. John baptized for forgiveness of sins. Jesus had none to forgive.

Why was he baptized?

The only reason he gives to John is "to fulfill all righteousness." What does that mean? Is it equivalent to, "It's just the right thing to do?" No, I think it's more than that. Did he mean, "I have to do all that God requires?" Certainly that was true. Jesus did come to do the will of his Father. But even more is meant here.

"To fulfill all righteousness." How was the righteousness of God ultimately fulfilled? Was it not on the cross? Paul says, "God made him who had no sin to be sin for us, so that in him we might become the righteousness of God" (2 Corinthians 5:21). The steps of Jesus into the waters of baptism were his first steps to the cross. He was baptized, not for his own sins, but for ours. Years before, Isaiah the prophet had spoken of the Suffering Servant of God as one "numbered with the transgressors." God "made him to be sin for us." When did this happen? Certainly on the cross. But when was the first time that Jesus identified with sinners? What did he do that only sinners do?

He was baptized.

In Jesus' mind baptism was always linked with the cross. He himself saw his baptism as a step toward death. James and John ask to sit on his right and left in glory. "'You don't know what you are asking,' Jesus said. 'Can you drink the cup I drink or be baptized with the baptism I am baptized with?'" (Mark 10:38). Jesus had long before been baptized with water. Now he looked toward the baptism of the cross. Later, he says, "But I have a baptism to undergo, and how distressed I am until it is completed!" (Luke 12:50).

Baptism and death. They always go together. Jesus saves us by his death on the cross, but that death is prefigured in his baptism. He died for us. He was baptized for us. Our sins drove him to the baptismal water just as they cost him his own blood and water.

Jesus is one of us. A sinner. Not with his own sins, but ours. He comes to John to wash those sins away, to bring in the righteousness of God.

Baptized with Jesus

"We were therefore buried with him through baptism into death. . . ."

Romans 6:4a

What does it mean to be baptized in Jesus' name? Is it just a ceremonial pronouncement made at baptism, "I baptize you in the name of the Father and of the Son and of the Holy Spirit?" Yes, but it is much more than that. To be baptized in his name is to be forgiven by his authority. The authority of the One who became sin for us. The power of the cross.

What's more, to be baptized in his name means we are baptized with him. Paul tells the Romans they had died to sin in baptism:

> Or don't you know that all of us who were baptized into Christ Jesus were baptized into his death? We were therefore buried with him through baptism into death in order

> that, just as Christ was raised from the dead through the glory of the Father, we too may live a new life.
>
> If we have been united with him like this in his death, we will certainly also be united with him in his resurrection.
>
> Romans 6:3-5

Jesus is baptized. We are baptized with him. What happened to him happens to us. Do you remember your baptism? Even if those memories aren't too clear, I can tell you what happened to you because I know what happened to Jesus.

When you were baptized the heavens opened. You might not have seen it with the naked eye, but they were opened and innumerable blessings came down.

When you were baptized, the Spirit descended. No dove may have been spotted, but the Spirit came nevertheless, the Spirit promised to all who repent and are baptized (Acts 2:38). The Spirit who brings new life.

When you were baptized, a voice from heaven spoke. No ear may have heard it, but you heard it in your heart. The voice said to you as it said to Jesus, "You are my child; I am pleased with you."

Were our baptisms exactly like Jesus' baptism? No. No more than our crosses are exactly like his. But we were baptized with him as certainly as we died with him.

And that baptism continues. Although I was quite young when I was baptized, I'll never forget how I felt immediately afterward. I had an overwhelming sense of being clean, of being right with God and others. My heart was singing. Perhaps you have the same memories and wonder why you don't feel that way now. If only we could be baptized again and again to know and feel we are clean before God.

But there is no need for that. Baptism is once for all. It's a permanent cleansing. We might understand that better if we changed the way we talk about baptism. "Have you been baptized?" we ask people. "Yes," they reply, "I have been baptized."

It would be better if we talked of baptism like we talk of another permanent commitment, marriage. You ask me, "Are you married?" I reply, "I have been married." What kind of impression would that answer give? Wouldn't you think me widowed or (more likely) divorced? Now the truth is I have been married. It's been a long time since my wedding and my memories are hazy regarding that event, but I assure you, I have been married by a preacher and before witnesses. My answer, "I have been married," is therefore true.

True, but misleading. It's not just that I have been through a marriage ceremony, but more importantly, that I *am* married. Happily so, if case you wonder. Those vows I made many years ago changed my identity. I am now Deb's husband. Two became one. Those vows brought me into a new family.

It's the same way with baptism. It's true that we who are Christians have been baptized. True, but misleading. It makes it sound as if baptism was some ritual in our past that has little meaning for us now. It would better if we said, "I *am* baptized." Baptized with Jesus. In his Name. Into his death. United with his resurrection. Our baptism is once and for all. There we made our vows to cling to him alone. We became united with him. We came into a new family. Forever. Even if it means we go to the cross with him. And we will.

But these vows not even death can sever.

DAY 5

Strange Temptations

Matthew 4:1-11

Jesus is baptized. He receives the Spirit. Immediately the Spirit leads him. Leads him to the wilderness. Leads him to temptation.

How can this be? How can the Spirit of the God of love lead Jesus and lead us to be tempted? Note that the devil, not the Spirit, does the actual temptation. God tempts no one. He wants us to resist sin. Yet out of his great love for us, God sent his Son to be a man, to be human. To be human is to be tempted. The Spirit leads Jesus and he sometimes leads us to the test, not to make us sin but to make us stronger. Still, we know our limitations and we pray, "Lead us not into temptation, but deliver us from the evil one" (Matthew 6:13).

Jesus was tempted. Really tempted. It was no act, no "put-on." He was tempted as we are.

What does it mean to be tempted? It means part of us wants to do what is wrong. If we have no desire to do wrong, we cannot be tempted. So it was with Jesus. He was human. Part of him wanted to do what was wrong. If not, then he was not really tempted.

Does this shock us? Can we admit that Jesus was really tempted? Or do we have a false view of Jesus, one that cannot believe he was tempted like we are? The real Jesus was tempted. The Bible says so. He was flesh and blood. This means there was the possibility that Jesus would sin. If not, then there was no real temptation. But God cannot sin. How can this be?

It's one of the great mysteries of faith and a shocking demonstration of God's love. God cared so much for us that he put his very nature in jeopardy by sending his Son to be tempted. If Satan had won this battle with Jesus, then God would not be God. He would not be the Holy God of Scripture. As Jesus, God in the flesh, confronts Satan, the universe holds its breath at the outcome.

What did the temptation look like? Did the devil just come to Jesus and say, "Hi, I'm Satan. Do these things"? Perhaps, but I don't think so. How did Satan tempt Jesus? The same way he tempts us. Have you ever heard the voice of the devil? Of course we have. We hear it in our own head and hearts. We have desires that look good at the moment but on further reflection lead us away from our Father. This is one area where we find it easy to relate to Jesus. We know temptation, so it should not be too difficult to imagine ourselves with him in the desert.

Meeting Needs

"... for forty days he was tempted by the devil." Luke 4:2a

Forty days without food is a long time. It's not humanly impossible; longer fasts have been done, but it seems beyond the power of most.

But not Jesus. For forty days he had been without food. He was hungry. Hungrier than I have ever been. So hungry, he looked for something, anything to eat.

Even at the rocks. A voice said, "Turn them to bread." He could have. He had the power. He wanted to. He was hungry.

He didn't.

"Why not?" we may ask. What would have been so wrong with Jesus turning stones,to bread? Where's the harm? Did God want him to be hungry?

And there's the answer. Jesus quotes part of a passage from Deuteronomy. Another part of that passage says because God loved the Israelites he caused them to be hungry. The whole idea may shock us. Doesn't God want to bless us? Doesn't he want to fulfill our every need? How can a loving Father deny his children?

What truly loving father does *not* deny his children. Kids don't know what's good for them. On their own they'd eat nothing but junk food. When I was a kid and refused to eat my supper because there was something I didn't like, my dad always had the same answer: "Let him alone; he'll eat when he's hungry enough."

It's the same way with our heavenly Father. We don't know how to be hungry. We hunger for all the junk foods of life--money, sex, power, recognition, happiness--instead of hungering for what is truly good and satisfying. God wanted Israel to hunger for him alone. Jesus had learned that lesson. Have we?

The Power of Publicity

". . . throw yourself down. . . ." Matthew 4:6b

Then the devil took Jesus to the pinnacle of the temple and said, "Jump."

This is a strange temptation. Why should Jesus want to jump off the temple?

Satan says, "If you do, angels will lift you up in their hands." What Jesus confronts here is the ultimate publicity stunt, the greatest evangelistic technique ever devised. By jumping and being caught by angels, all in Jerusalem would have proof that Jesus was indeed the Son of God. Satan expresses the doubts of those unbelievers: "*If* you are the Son of God, throw yourself down."

So what was the harm? Many in the church today would urge Jesus to jump, perhaps would even nudge him a little. After all, shouldn't we do anything it takes to get people to believe?

But Jesus says no. To get believers through technique is not faithfulness; it is a sin. It is idolatry, relying on our own devices, not on the God who calls sinners to faith. "Do not put the Lord your God to the test." So Jesus said.

There is a vast difference between trusting God and testing God. Jesus trusted his Father completely; he knew he would save him if he jumped off the temple. But trust is shown in obedience, not in testing. To test God is to attempt to control him, to manipulate him, to put him on a leash. The God of Hosts will not be tamed. It is blasphemy to try. We cannot control him. The world is in his hands. He is Lord. We are not. To be faithful to this Lord is not always to be successful. Trust, sometimes leads to defeat, even to a cross. Jesus was tempted to take the easy way out, to gain notoriety and converts with the ultimate publicity stunt.

Today in our rush to solve problems in the church, to grow, to meet needs, to be relevant, we run the risk of trusting technique, not God, thereby becoming ultimately irrelevant. In one city there is a religious group that tries everything it can to draw people: newspaper ads, comfortable buildings, celebrity speakers, economic growth seminars, every technique imaginable. It's called "The Church of Today."

If we are not very careful, that's what we can become. Not a church with a past, upholding a tradition of faithfulness throughout the centuries. Not a church with a future, creating faithful persons who pass on the gospel story to a new generation. Simply the church of today, subject to whatever fashion happens to be popular.

By jumping off the temple, Jesus could have been the "Messiah of today." His ministry could have been popular and painless. But he knew the will of the Father was driving him not to technique, but to the cross.

There will always be someone who has the solution to our problems, the right technique for growth and evangelism. But the Bible offers no technique but the old tried-and-true one— faithful, humble, sacrificial service. "If anyone would come after me, he must deny himself and take up his cross daily and follow me." There is our technique.

Or so said Jesus.

Having It All

". . . showed him all the kingdoms of the world and their splendor."

Matthew 4:8b

"Who says you can't have it all?" So went an old television commercial. Our culture tells us we can have it all: good family life, successful career, comfortable living, and a pleasant retirement. We are constantly bombarded with the message that we should want more. We believe it a sin in our society to settle for less, to be less than we can be, to stop reaching for another goal, another experience.

Who says we can't have it all?

God says. He even said it to Jesus.

Jesus found himself on a very high mountain. Stretching below him, he could see the cities of Judea. In his mind's eye, he could see the splendor of the great cities of the world: Rome, with its golden palaces; Alexandria, with its bustling markets; Athens, with its marble temples. It was heady stuff for a poor boy from Nazareth. "All this can be yours," he heard.

It was tempting. Who wouldn't want to be king of the world? Think of the good he could do. He could feed the poor, end corruption in government, bring health care to all. If the world were his, it'd be a better world.

And he deserved it. Who says he shouldn't have all the kingdoms of the world? They belonged to him already! He was the Son of God, the Creator. All he needed to do was to take possession of what already was his.

But he didn't. For he knew this was not God's way of taking possession. All the world would be his, but only after the cross. Only after the resurrection. Only on that final day when every knee would bow and every tongue confess his name. He knew to take possession now would mean to serve the lord of this age, so he said, "Away from me, Satan! For it is written: 'Worship the Lord your God and serve him only.'"

Like Israel, Jesus is tempted to lose patience. When Moses goes upon the mountain to get the commandments, he is gone for forty days. While Moses waits on the mountain for the first two commandments: "You will have no other gods before me" and "You shall not make for yourself an idol. . ." (Exodus 20:3-4), the Israelites impatiently make an idol and call it their god. They want their needs met now. They will not wait for God to act in his own time.

Jesus faces the same temptation. Satan promises the kingdoms now, not after the cross. Where Israel fails, Jesus proves faithful. He will serve God alone. He will wait for the Father to act, even if that waiting means suffering and death.

Jesus would not sell his soul for all the world. Would you? Would I? Many sell theirs for much less. We give ourselves to "having it all" or at least to having more, and we forget the high price we pay. No Christian would literally bow down and worship Satan. Yet by wanting the things of this world, wanting success and happiness and pleasure, we serve this world's lord.

Isn't this God's world? Doesn't God want us to be happy? Of course, but he knows the things of this world will not satisfy. As God's children, we are in exactly the same situation as Jesus. All the world is God's and all the world is ours. But not yet. The day will come when we reign with Christ in a new heaven and a new earth, but now is not the time to reign. In this life we are to have tribulation. The meek will inherit the earth, but not on Satan's terms, not even on their own terms—only if they worship the Lord God alone.

Who says we can't have it all? God does. Not in this life. He even warns us that what we already have may be too much. Already our knees may be bent a bit in homage to the one who promises success but ultimately can't deliver. To him we too must shout, "Away from us, Satan." And we must turn again to serve the only One who truly satisfies.

DAY 6

The Master Teacher

Luke 4:16-30; 8:9-10

Anyone who teaches knows how hard it is to make the lesson both clear and interesting. I grew up hearing that Jesus was the master teacher. He came to make clear God's ways to humans. He used familiar illustrations, parables, so that even his slowest students could understand him. If only those who teach today in our schools and churches would follow his example and make their lessons simple and easy.

This picture of Jesus as a teacher is false. Completely false. The usual reaction to his teaching was not, "Aha, now I understand," but "What do these things mean?" He said he used parables not to make things clear, but to hide them from the hard-hearted. He constantly frustrated his students (called disciples in the New Testament), forcing them to stay after school and ask him for help. They just didn't get it.

So is Jesus the master teacher? Yes, but his listeners were not amazed because of his teaching techniques but because he taught with authority (Matthew 7:29). If we find his teachings comfortable and easily understood, chances are we have missed the whole point. His words are meant to turn us upside down. They revolutionize our thinking and our lives. "This is a hard saying," his contemporaries complained, "who can hear it?"

We, on the other hand, are more likely to react to his teachings with, "This is an old saying, and everybody has heard it." The words of Jesus are so familiar to us that we think we have them all figured out.

We don't. It may be harder for us to hear him and understand than it was for his contemporaries. At least they knew they needed help. We don't even realize how radical his message is. Can we even begin to see the world as he saw it? Can we break out of our lethargy to even want to understand?

How Not to Hold an Audience

"All spoke well of him. . . ." Luke 4:22a

Jesus had them in the palm of his hand.

It was quite an occasion for him. He had returned home the conquering hero. Word of his powerful preaching spread throughout Galilee; every synagogue was abuzz with stories of his exploits.

So he came to Nazareth, his hometown, and was asked to speak at the synagogue. No doubt his family was there, sitting proudly on the front pew. You could see his boyhood companions elbowing their friends and saying, "I knew him when he was a nobody." Everyone spoke well of him. He had them in the palm of his hand.

Then Jesus blew it. He went out of his way to offend the Nazarenes. They turn quickly from approval to attempted murder, running him out of town and threatening to throw him off a cliff.

What did Jesus say? What made them so angry? He turned from a word of promise to a word of judgment. "The year of the Lord's favor is here," he said, and all applauded. "But you will not accept the Lord's prophet," he added, and all were filled with rage. Jesus came with good news: "Salvation has come." But not good news for everyone. For some, it was the worst news possible because they would not believe and obey the Savior. So they reacted in typical fashion: If you don't like the news, kill the messenger.

What makes a preacher successful? If we follow Jesus' example, a successful preacher is one who gets fired from his job, run out of town, and threatened with death. Some of the early preachers, Paul in particular, learned that lesson well.

More importantly, what makes a successful church? The problem at Nazareth wasn't with the preacher but with his congregation. Certainly we should not follow the example of the Nazarene synagogue. If we are to hear the truth of Christ's words of judgment, we must react to them not with anger, but with repentance.

Jesus didn't know how to hold an audience. He told them the truth. God grant that those who preach also have the courage to tell the truth. And that we who hear have the courage to listen.

How to Confuse Your Students

"... I speak in parables, so that, 'though seeing they may not see; though hearing, they may not understand.'" Luke 8:10b

I began preaching when I was a teenager. You can imagine how bad some of those early sermons must have been. Once I was asked to preach for a nearby congregation. After the sermon, the regular preacher there got up and said, "I think we all know what Gary was trying to say." Ever since then, I've realized that the best I can do is to try to say something and hope the congregation understands. If only I could communicate as clearly as Jesus.

Only Jesus did not make things clear. He confused his students. He taught in parables not to simplify the gospel with appropriate illustrations, but to intentionally obscure. "I speak so they may not understand," he said. What kind of good teaching is this? Don't good teachers do everything to make their students understand? Why would any teacher intentionally make his lesson hard to fathom?

Was Jesus a bad teacher?

If teaching is measured by the number of simple facts memorized, the answer is, "Yes, he was a bad teacher." It was not Jesus' purpose to get the crowds to pass a test on his teachings. His purpose was to separate believer from unbeliever, disciple from crowd, sheep from goat. His gospel was not a simple teaching, easy to grasp. It was a difficult gospel, difficult to understand and even more difficult to follow. "How hard it is to enter the kingdom," Jesus said.

It's not that some of his hearers were smart and some were dumb. All were dumb. All had the learning disability called "sin." None could grasp the kingdom of God. But God in his grace gave some "the secrets of the kingdom of God" (Luke 8:10). Being a disciple is not a matter of intellectually mastering certain material. It is a matter of being completely mastered, body, soul, heart, and intellect, by God.

What does this say to us as hearers of the gospel? It is a strong warning. If we think we completely understand Jesus, we need to think again. He taught in parables to confuse those who wanted easy answers. To confuse, but also to prompt them to ask, "What does this mean?" As we study the Bible we too must constantly ask, "What does this mean?" not just intellectually, but what does it mean for our lives. How does this word judge us? Who is this Savior we are called to follow? What does he demand? Are we willing to pay the cost of discipleship?

If we ask, we too will be given the kingdom's secrets.

DAY
7

A Nice Little Miracle

John 2:1-11

The Wedding

It was a small wedding in a small town in a small corner of the world. The bride and groom were like countless others who had gone before. The ceremony was traditional with no surprises. The problem came with the wedding feast.

As was the custom, the feast was an elaborate affair, lasting for days and involving everyone in the village. Preparations had been underway for weeks—women stood over boiling cook pots, men set up tables in the town square, even the children were busy gathering wildflowers for decorations. Finally all was ready.

The bride and groom and the wedding guests arrived. All had plenty to eat and drink. This pleased the man in charge, the master of the feast.

Then disaster struck. A servant went to a wine jar and found it empty. No problem. He'd just find another. But it was empty too, as was the next, and the next. What was he to do? Run to the master of the feast and say, "We've run out of wine?" The master would be furious. No wedding was complete without wine. The guests would soon complain. The bride and groom would face embarrassment. The one perfect day of their lives would be forever ruined.

The servant did not know what to do. He had no money to buy wine. Even if he did, the closest village was miles away and he couldn't get there and back before the feast ended. What could he do? Nothing but tell the master of the feast the truth. There was no more wine.

However, a kind woman was there, a guest from Nazareth. He mentioned the problem to her, and she mentioned it to her son. At first he seemed reluctant to help, "Why do you involve me?" he asked his mother. But the woman told the servant, "Do whatever my son tells you."

All fine and good, but what could her son, Jesus, do? Where could he find wine for all these people? "You see those six jars over there?" Jesus told the servant, "Fill them with water."

The jars in question were huge, each holding twenty to thirty gallons. So the servant called his fellow workers and they filled the jars. It made no sense, but what could they lose?

"Draw out some water and take it to the master of the banquet," Jesus said.

"This will never work," thought the servant. "Does this Jesus really think the master can't tell water from wine?" But in his desperation, he did what Jesus commanded.

"Here you are master, more wine for you to taste." As the master tasted the water, the servant cowered, expecting a blow for trying to fool him so obviously. But he finished the cup and smiled. "This is the best wine I've ever tasted," he said, complimenting the groom for his generosity. As the servant took the cup, he looked inside. It was wine! He couldn't believe it! He took a sip himself. It was true!

By one small act this Jesus had turned the wedding from a disaster to a complete success.

The First Miracle

John tells us this was the first "sign" or miracle that Jesus performed. It's not what we might expect as the first miracle. After all, wouldn't we expect Jesus to begin his ministry with a bang? We want a dramatic and public miracle, maybe healing someone blind from birth or walking on water or even raising someone from the dead. We expect a miracle that everyone knows about and no one can deny, so that everyone will come to believe in Jesus.

Instead Jesus gives us a nice little miracle. A miracle, to be sure, to take ordinary water and turn it into the best wine, 120 to 150 gallons of it! Still, it was a miracle that few saw. The guests are unaware that anything strange had happened. The master of the feast marvels only at the quality of the wine. Who even knew a miracle had taken place? Mary, the servants, Jesus, and his disciples. How do we know the disciples knew? John tells us, "This, the first of his miraculous signs, Jesus performed in Cana of Galilee. He thus revealed his glory, and his disciples put their faith in him" (John 2:11).

So why begin a ministry with such a quiet miracle? Perhaps because, as Jesus told Mary, his time had not yet come. The day would come when Jesus would heal the blind and raise the dead, when all would confront the question of his identity, when the choice to follow him or crucify him would be clear. For now, Jesus was content to raise a small band of followers, the disciples. This small sign was for them, so they would put their faith in him.

Signs by their very nature point to things beyond themselves. So too, this sign of Jesus points to God the Father. What can we learn about our heavenly Father from a wedding feast long ago?

A God of Little Things

Our God is an awesome God. He is the Lord of Hosts, the Creator of the Universe, and the King of Kings. The far-flung planets, the wind and waves, the burning flames of the angels—he commands them all with a single word.

Can such a God care for us? We can imagine him dealing with presidents and kings, with the wealthy and powerful, with the rich and famous. But can he care for ordinary people, like you and me? Can we even imagine that the Almighty King of the Universe can take the time to deal with the problems of people like us, nobodies that the world doesn't notice?

"I'm not a nobody," you may say, "I'm a very important person." Are you? Who knows you beyond your circle of family, friends, and business acquaintances? Do you own a business? Good and well, but won't it continue when you're gone? Do your children love you? Wonderful, but will your great-grandchildren even remember your name? At times, we may be impressed by our importance, but in our saner moments we know that we are ordinary people, "just plain folks," who will never be on television, never meet the president, never have a candy bar named after us.

Can the Almighty care for us? Indeed, he does. He cared enough to send his Son for us. He sent him, not in trappings of fame and glory, but to an ordinary girl in an ordinary town. Born, not in a palace, but in a stable. Wrapped, not in royal robes, but in humble strips of cloth. Not on a throne, but in a manger. In the face of Christ, we see a God who cares for ordinary people.

His Son cared enough to go to an ordinary wedding at an ordinary town and do an extraordinary thing. To insure the joy of the most important day of their lives, he turned water into wine. This same Jesus has the power to turn our hours and days, whether ordinary or important, into times where his power and glory are seen.

Even three o'clock on Tuesday can be a sign that points to the God who cares, the God for whom there are no little towns, little things, or little people.

A God of Celebration

Religious people have a reputation for being a joyless lot. Today, when you tell people you're a Christian they sometimes react with, "Well, I'll have to watch my language," or "Then I guess they'll be no fun around here." Since some forms of worldly "fun" are sinful, those around us assume Christians condemn all enjoyment. Christians are always serious, always judgmental, always spoiling the fun.

It was the same in Jesus' day. The religious people, the scribes and the Pharisees, were certainly serious folk. They clearly condemned the ungodliness of their time. They kept the commandments faithfully. They fasted often. To them, the joys of the world were snares to avoid. They followed God, not pleasure.

Which is one reason, they opposed Jesus. He didn't take his religion seriously enough! He didn't fast like the Pharisees and John the Baptist. He was always breaking the rules the Pharisees had made to protect the Law. He even enjoyed weddings and parties with unacceptable people. He even turned water into wine! No wonder his contemporaries called him "a glutton and a drunkard, a friend of tax collectors and 'sinners'" (Matthew 11:19).

Jesus turned water into wine. Not a little water and a little wine, but a prodigious amount: 120 to 180 gallons of it. Jesus knew how to celebrate the God of abundance. He came to give not just an abundance of wine, but an abundance of life: "I have come that they may have life, and have it abundantly" (John 10:10 NRSV). In this small act in a small town we catch a glimpse of the God who "is able to accomplish abundantly far more than we can ask or imagine" (Ephesians 3:20). Jesus teaches us how to enjoy the abundance of God.

In light of the abuse of alcohol in our society, abstinence may be the best policy for Christians. But we are disloyal to Jesus if we let our abstinence from alcohol sour our entire outlook on life in this world. Christians alone are the true party animals, inviting others to the greatest party of all: the eternal kingdom of God where there is always laughter and no tears. We do the world a disservice if we let them think Christians are boring or prudes or party-poopers.

Jesus liked parties. He even brought the wine.

The God of Transformation

Jesus took the most ordinary thing in the world, plain old water, and transformed it into the extraordinary, the best wine. I don't think it is reading too much into the story to see more here than a simple chemical change. What Jesus did at Cana, he can do in each of us. He takes our ordinary, plain, humdrum lives and transforms them into something new, something special. With Jesus in us, even the ordinary tasks of life become meaningful, for we do them in his name and to his glory.

So this sign reminds us of the God we serve. He and he alone can make things new in our lives. God promises a truly new deal: forgiveness of sin, a law in our hearts, and knowledge of the Lord himself. All come from God's initiative and action, not from our human efforts to do something new. God will do "new things, hidden things that you have not known" (Isaiah 48:6). He will give us a new name (Isaiah 62:2), changing things so radically that it will be like making a new heaven and a new earth (Isaiah 66:22). God promises a new start, a fresh beginning.

That promise becomes true in Jesus. He comes as something old, the Messiah, the one the Jews had expected for centuries. But something is new about his coming, so new that those who looked for the Messiah couldn't see him when he came. When God sends something new, it truly is new; so new we fail to recognize it. So new we may even fight against it.

So Jesus' contemporaries didn't understand the new thing God was doing among them. They criticized Jesus for not following the old paths: "Why do your disciples eat and drink, when the disciples of John and those of the Pharisee's fast and pray?" In answer, Jesus unveiled the new:

> He also told them a parable: "No one tears a piece of cloth from a new garment and sews it on an old garment; otherwise the new will be torn, and the piece from the new will not match the old. And no one puts new wine into old wineskins; otherwise the new wine will burst the skins and will be spilled, and the skins will be destroyed. But new wine must be put into fresh wineskins." Luke 5:36-38

When the disciples saw Jesus turn the water into wine, they saw a sign that pointed them to a greater truth: This Jesus shares in the very nature of God, he has God's glory. Like God the Father, he cares for those the world ignores. Like God, he gives abundantly. Like God, he has the power to change the ordinary into the extraordinary.

As we look at his miracle two millennia later, may we also see more than just a nice little miracle. We see in this small act the Jesus who cares, who gives, who changes us. That change, like the miracle, takes place in obedience. "Do whatever he tells you," Mary told the servants. And they did. By his power and through their obedience the water becomes wine. In the same way, it is not our power but his that changes us, yet this power comes through a long obedience. May we each day see signs of his glory in our lives and respond by doing whatever he wills.

Then we too will truly be his disciples.

DAY 8

Go Fish!

Luke 5:1-11

Skydiving. Mountain climbing. Auto racing. Chainsaw juggling. What do they have in common?

All are dangerous sports. In each there is always a good chance one may lose life or limb. This possibility of injury gives these sports at least part of their appeal. In them one courts danger, living on the edge, looking death in the face and laughing.

A Dangerous Sport

"Put out into deep water, and let down the nets for a catch." Luke 5:4b

What are other dangerous sports? How about fishing?

There was once a group of professional fisherman who got more than they bargained for on their fishing expedition. In the middle of doing what they had done day after day and time after time, they suddenly ran into something more startling and surprising than a bank. They too have their world turned upside down.

It all started like an ordinary day, or rather an ordinary night. Peter and his partners, James and John, prepared their nets, got into their boats, and cast off for some night fishing. They were professional fishermen like their fathers and grandfathers before them. They knew the Sea of Galilee like the back of their hands, knew where the fish would be and when they would be there. They cast their nets with elegance as if they were extensions of their bodies. Then they sat in the boat to wait. They knew how to wait. They knew how to fish. This was their life.

So they waited. And waited. And waited some more. Finally John suggested they try another spot. Grunting with the effort, they pulled the nets back into the boat, cast off, and rowed. "This is where they'll be," said James. Back into the water went the nets. Back to waiting went the fisherman. They knew how to wait.

Still no fish. So they try another spot. And another. And another. Soon the sky begins to lighten. Day breaks. Still no fish.

Tired, frustrated, and disappointed, they return to shore. Dragging their boats onto land, they begin to wash and fold their nets. "We'll try again tonight," Peter says.

The Obedient Disciple

Their work is interrupted by a crowd. "What are so many people doing at the lakeside this morning?" they think. Then they spot Jesus. "Ah," they say, "so that's it. They've all come to hear the new rabbi."

The crowd is so eager to hear Jesus, they push him to the edge of the lake. Seeing Peter's boat, he steps inside. "Simon," he says, "push the boat a little from the shore." So Simon pushes the boat and jumps in beside Jesus who teaches the people from the boat. "I never thought my boat would be a pulpit," thinks Peter.

Jesus teaches the crowd for quite some time. Peter's mind wanders from fatigue. After all, he'd been working all night. Suddenly Peter hears Jesus call his name. "What, Lord?" he says.

"I'm through teaching for today," says Jesus. "Let's go fishing. Put out in the deep water and let down your nets."

"What a time for a fishing trip!" mused Peter. "I'm sick of fishing. Besides, this Jesus is no fisherman. He's just a carpenter and a rabbi. A fishing boat is no place for a preacher. He can bless the boat, but if he comes with us he might hear some language he wouldn't hear in the synagogue. Furthermore, if we didn't catch anything all night, what makes him think he can? But he is the Teacher and he did heal my mother-in-law, so I owe him one."

So he says, "Master, we've worked hard all night and haven't caught a thing, but if you say so, I'll let down the nets."

At this point, Peter's faith is tested. Peter is a fisherman, a professional. Jesus is not. When it comes to fishing, can we blame Peter for thinking he knows more than Jesus?

Do we ever think we know more than Jesus? Do we ever accuse him of meddling in areas where he is no expert? How many of us confine our Christianity to one day, Sunday, or one place, the church? "Religion's fine," we say, "in its place." But if the preacher or Bible teacher implies that the principles of Jesus should rule our lives at work on Monday, we think they've gone too far. What does Jesus know about business? "Turn the other cheek" may work for the preacher, but he doesn't live in the dog-eat-dog world we live in. In our world if you turn the other cheek you just get knocked down again.

So we try to confine Jesus to the ghetto called "Religion." Just keep him there where he belongs. But our chains won't hold him. He keeps meddling in areas that don't concern him. He thinks he should be the Lord of every part of our lives. He even ties to tell Peter how to fish.

But Peter is an obedient disciple. Against his inclination and better judgment, he does what Jesus says. He lowers the nets.

What happens astounds him. Where there had been no fish the night before, there now are hundreds. The nets begin to break! "James, John, come quickly!" he shouts. With great effort they haul up the nets and fill both boats so full they begin to sink beneath the weight.

The Sinful Servant

Peter sees all this and reacts violently. Falling at the feet of Jesus, he cries, "Get away from me, Lord; I am a sinful man!"

Why such an extreme reaction? True, this is an amazing miracle, but just before this Jesus had healed Peter's mother-in-law from fever. Peter did not react so strongly then, why does he do so now?

Because Jesus has invaded Peter's home turf (or rather, home surf). When Jesus heals his mother-in-law, Peter is impressed, but after all, maybe Jesus just knows more about healing than Peter does. Peter is no physician.

He is a fisherman. He knows how and where and when to catch fish. But now Jesus has invaded his territory. Peter, James, and John had worked all night, catching nothing. They were professionals. If they caught no fish, then there were none to be caught.

Yet Jesus comes and with a word catches more fish than Peter had ever seen at one time. Suddenly Peter saw Jesus as he'd never seen him before. The power in Jesus couldn't be contained in words like "religion" or "teaching" or even "healing." It was a power over all. The power of God himself.

So Peter reacts strongly. We understand that. But we expect him to say, "Lord, how powerful you are!" or "Lord, I tremble before one who can do such things." Why does he react with these words: "Depart from me, I am a sinner"? Is this just another example of Peter's impulsiveness? Does he just blurt out the first thing that comes to mind?

No. These are very appropriate words. Peter has caught a glimpse of the power of God in Jesus. He has seen Jesus for who he is: the Holy One of God. Only God himself who made the world, the sea, and all within it could call forth such a catch. Here in a small boat in a small lake in a small corner of the world is God himself. The earth cannot contain him, much less Peter's boat.

What do we do in the presence of a Holy God and a Holy Jesus? What do we do when we see Jesus where we least expect him—not at church but on our turf? When we see his power in our families, at our jobs, in school, even at play? When he muscles into those areas where we think we are professionals?

We bow. In fear, in repentance, we fall at his feet. We are ruined, for he is Holy God and we are unclean. He amazes us and scares us with what he has done, what he can do.

The Fisher of Men

Peter falls at Jesus' feet, a sinner. He is raised by Jesus with the words "Don't be afraid; from now on you will catch men" (Luke 5:10). The forgiveness Jesus gives frees Peter from the bondage and fear sin brings. It frees him to hear the call to catch others.

"Catching people" is a strange term for evangelism. After all, we catch fish for our own good, not the good of the fish. But the Greek word for "catch" here means "to capture alive." Peter is called, not to bring death to fish, but to bring life to people. This metaphor of fishing for proclaiming God's will is therefore not so strange. It also has its roots in the Old Testament prophets, although there it usually is a picture of God's judgment on evil.

Peter's call is different. The one who calls him came into the world not "to condemn the world, but to save the world. . ."(John 3:17). He hooks men, not to clean them for eating, but to clean them from sin. He rescues them alive from the deep waters of guilt and despair.

Peter, James, and John are called to this task of fishing for men. They hear the call, but it is not without cost. They pull their boats to shore, then leave everything to follow Jesus.

It's a disturbing picture. "They left everything and followed him." They leave two boats full of fish to rot in the sunshine. They had worked all night for fish and gotten nothing. Now they have more fish than they can imagine and they leave it all behind. They leave fish and family and profession and all that is familiar to them to follow this stranger. Why? Because in him they have seen more than fish, more than family, more than familiarity and comfort. They have seen power. They have seen holiness. They have seen God.

We too are called to fish for people, to capture them alive for Jesus. We call it evangelism. No word frightens Christians more than "evangelism." Why does it frighten us? Perhaps it reminds us of older evangelism techniques—knocking on doors, passing out tracts, bussing them in—that didn't work. Perhaps it reminds us of times we tried to share our faith and came away embarrassed. Perhaps it seems like meddling to question the spiritual state of others. Perhaps it's just too hard. We don't want to do it.

What will move us to overcome our fear of evangelism? Only a greater fear. Peter sees the great catch of fish that comes at Jesus' command. It scares him to death. It scares him because he is in the presence of the power of God. What will move us to catch people? Fear. Fear of Jesus. Not the fear he will condemn us if we don't evangelize, but that holy fear that sees him as he is. If we but glimpse his power in every moment of our lives, then nothing else can scare us. If we hear his voice say, "Don't be afraid," then we are ready to tell others of his grace. If we hear his command, "Go, catch people," then we know he gives us the power to reel them in.

We must cast our nets for people. To do so requires effort. It may even require sleepless nights of toil. It requires we leave everything, as these disciples did. It requires we risk ridicule, embarrassment, and hurt feelings to share the gospel.

We must cast our nets for people, but we rely not on our own abilities for success. We rely on the powerful Lord. Sometimes we may not know where to cast. The Lord may call those whom we consider the least likely converts. We must cast where he leads. At times we may grow discouraged at our lack of success. We may go days, weeks, and months without a nibble. We should never be discouraged, knowing that we are faithful disciples. We are obedient disciples who launch into the deep at the command of our Lord, knowing he came to catch people.

Not with a hook, but with a cross.

DAY
9

Just Dropped In

Luke 5:17-26

"We have seen remarkable things today." Luke 5:26b

Last night on the news I saw another story about yet another lawsuit. Litigation seems to be our national pastime. In this case, a group of disabled citizens was suing a local business for not providing handicapped access to their stores, as is mandated by the Americans with Disabilities Act.

But perhaps this lawsuit had merit. What would it be like to be disabled, to be chained (as it were) to a wheelchair? To be robbed of abilities that most of us don't even think about? The ability to go where we want, do what we want? The ability to work? Even the ability to wash and shave and feed ourselves? What must it be like to be at the mercy of family or friends or strangers? Is it too much to ask that we be allowed to enter public places of business like everyone else?

Like you, I have friends and acquaintances who are wheelchair bound. Most of the time I don't even notice because they are so adept at coping with their situation. But at times they must ask for help.

They must rely on others. Sometimes, even with help, it's not easy for them to get where they need to go.

A Man with Problems

There was a man who had a problem. Three problems to be exact.

For one, he was paralyzed. He couldn't move his hands and arms. An accident had stolen his normal life and for years he had to count on others. Unable to move. Unable to care for himself. He had to rely on his friends to bath him, shave him, feed him, and to take him anywhere he needed to go.

That was his second problem. He had heard a healer was coming to town, a rabbi named Jesus. This Jesus was rumored to have amazing powers. He had healed lepers, the lame, and the blind. The paralyzed man felt something he hadn't felt for years: hope. Hope that this Jesus could make well, that his life would be normal again. But how could he get to Jesus? He knew the house where he was teaching, but he couldn't get there.

A Man with Friends

Enter his four friends. They grab the corners of his bedroll and carry him to the house. He's fairly heavy; their arms strain with the effort, but they walk with smiles on their faces, knowing the rabbi will make their friend walk again.

But they face the third problem, the insurmountable one. The crowd is too large. It fills the house, spills out into the street, and blocks their way. "Excuse us." "Pardon." "Can we squeeze by?" they say, but it's no use, they can't get in. Their friend is doomed to a lifetime of paralysis. "Well, at least we tried," one thinks. "No one can accuse us of not caring about our friend."

Then another one of them looks up and points to the roof. The others look puzzled, but then understand. They manhandle their friend onto the roof, bed and all. One goes to find some rope. He returns and ties the rope to the corners of the bed, while the other three begin to dig through the baked clay.

Inside the house, Jesus is teaching. Caleb, the owner of the house, is as proud as he can be. The Master had agreed to come home with him, and what is more, the news had spread throughout the countryside. The greatest scholars of the law from Galilee, Judea, and Jerusalem had come to hear Jesus. Here they sat in Caleb's house! He could hardly believe it. "I must be the most envied man in the village today," he thought to himself.

Still, he hadn't figured on such a large crowd. They trampled his carpets, sat in the windows and doors, and pressed in so close one could hardly breathe. Funny though, Jesus didn't seem to mind the crowd, for he taught them and healed them with goodwill and patience.

Suddenly Caleb's musings are interrupted by a sound above him. Surely the crowd hadn't spilled over onto his roof. Jesus looks up too, but continues with his teaching.

Then they hear a scratching sound above them. "Mighty loud mice you have there, Caleb," Jesus says with a smile. Caleb returns an embarrassed smile, thinking, "What in the world can be going on?"

The scratching gets louder. "Maybe it's not mice, but goats you have up there, eh Caleb?"

Then the ceiling begins to cave in, showering Jesus and the other teachers with dust. Jesus takes it in stride, but some of the Pharisees look sternly at their host. Caleb is mortified.

Soon great chunks of clay rain down on their heads. Sunlight streams in and a face appears above them, then two, then three, then four.

"What's happening?" thinks Caleb. "Who's doing his to me, ruining what was the greatest day of my life?"

Suddenly all eyes turn upward as something descends into the room. "It's a man," someone whispers. "It's the one who is paralyzed," shouts another. Some in the crowd are amused. What a sight—to see a man on a mat lowered into a room by four ropes! Others hold their breath with anticipation. Many in the room are Pharisees, experts in the Law. They know their Bibles. They know that when the lame walk, the kingdom of God is near. So they wait to see what this Jesus will do. They wait to see if the kingdom has come.

The paralyzed man comes to rest at Jesus' feet. Jesus looks at him. He is not amused, but amazed. He marvels at the faith of the man's friends. What friends these must be, refusing to be defeated! Not settling for just a good effort, they found a way against all odds to bring the man to the healer. Jesus knows the crowd waits to see if the lame will leap. So Jesus gives the man what he needs.

A Man with a Savior

You see, the man had another problem. A problem far worse than pain, lack of mobility, or the press of the crowd. Jesus knew that problem.

"Friend, your sins are forgiven you."

"What is Jesus doing?" think some in the crowd. "The man needs healing, not forgiving. Make him walk, then worry about his sins."

The Pharisees and teachers of the law are shocked. They can't believe their ears! Does this Jesus really believe he has the power to forgive sins? God alone can forgive! Does this rabbi, this carpenter from Nazareth, believe he is God?

"Blasphemy! Blasphemy!" they cry. But only to themselves. Jesus is so popular with the crowd that they fear to say it out loud.

But Jesus knows what they're thinking.

"What makes you think these things?" he asks. "You've sat here and heard my teaching without correcting me. You've seen me heal person after person. Where do you think that teaching and that power come from? It can only come from God. If he gives me power to heal men's bodies, don't you think he gives me power to heal men's souls?"

So turning to the paralyzed man, Jesus says, "Get up, take your mat and go home."

The man begins to stir. The crowd gasps as he stands upright. He rolls up his mat, tucks it under his arm, and presses through the crowd. Praising God at the top of his lungs, he reaches the door. Tumbling down the stairs from the roof come his friends. He embraces them. Shoulder to shoulder they walk down the road toward home.

A day like no other day. This man regains his life. The friends see their loyalty rewarded beyond their dreams. The crowd see spectacle after spectacle. Teaching, healing, a man lowered through a roof, sins forgiven. They all go home saying, "We've seen remarkable things today."

Supporting Cast

An amazing day. An amazing story. Where do you find yourself in the story? Which character do you relate to?

Certainly we don't relate to the Pharisees. Or do we? The Pharisees were willing to accept Jesus as a fellow teacher of the Law. They are even willing to grant that he is a wonder-worker, a healer, one who does amazing miracles. They'd seen them with their own eyes. All this is fine. Jesus can teach the law and heal the sick and draw great crowds.

But he goes too far. He tells the paralytic, "Your sins are forgiven."

Suppose you visit a new church on Sunday. You sing. You pray. The service is no different from many you've been too. Suddenly a deacon announces, "If any of you want to confess your sins, please come forward and the pastor will forgive you." What would you think? "I must have misunderstood," you say to yourself. "He must have meant to say, 'Come forward, confess to God, and the pastor will help reassure you that God has heard your prayer.'" So you go to the deacon for clarification. He tells you, "I meant exactly what I said. Our pastor has the power to forgive sins."

Would you join that church? Would you even go back there again?

I don't think so, unless you went back to straighten them out. We are appalled that anyone would have the gall to think they can forgive sin. It's blasphemy! We can forgive those who sin against us. Only God can forgive when we sin against him.

That's exactly what the Pharisees said. Jesus forgives the paralytic's sins. Only God can forgive sin. Jesus therefore is either a blasphemous egomaniac claiming to be God or he is, in fact, God in the flesh. The Pharisees believed the first alternative. They were wrong.

Surely we are not like them. We are Christians. We confess Jesus as the Son of God, God incarnate. We know he can forgive sins. We rely on him to forgive ours.

But do we realize the enormity of that belief? Or, like the Pharisees, do we practically limit Jesus. He is our teacher. We feel comfortable with that. He heals the sick. We like that. Jesus is our friend. He is close to us. He knows how we feel because he suffered as we do. He too is human. We may forget he is much more. He is God, with all of God's holiness, justice, and wrath, as well as mercy. His ways are not our ways and we must approach him in reverence. Otherwise, like these Pharisees, we make him less than what he is.

We must not lose sight of the true hero of this story. At the center of the miracle is not the host, the friends, the Pharisees, or even the paralyzed man. At the center is Jesus. He is the hero of this story. Of every New Testament story. Of our story.

The point of this story? Jesus forgives sins. The greatest miracle performed that day was not the healing of one who was paralyzed; it was the forgiveness of a sinner. Jesus saves. It's an old lesson to most of us, so old we take it for granted. "Jesus saves." We see these words emblazoned on tee shirts, in neon on billboards, and handwritten on signs at football games. They are old words. Church words.

Jesus saves. Not *saved*, but *saves*. Our salvation is not just something we experienced long ago; it is an ever-present reality. His touch is as much in our lives now as it was on the day we accepted him as Lord. He said to the paralytic, "Your sins are forgiven." He said the same to us. He continues to say it, each moment of each day.

How many times do we see the problems in our lives—financial worries, poor health, depression, lack of friendship—and go to Jesus for help? Surely he has promised to give us what we need. We must fight the paralysis that keeps us from going to him. We must overcome the crowd, overcome any obstacle that stands in the way. We must dig through any barrier that separates us from him. But do we sometimes fail to see our greatest need? Do we fail to see his greatest gift?

"Your sins are forgiven."

That's just what we need to hear.

DAY
10

A Dangerous Rebel

Matthew 15:10-20; Luke 5:33-39; 6:1-5; John 5:39-47

We live in the time of the domesticated church. When one thinks of a dangerous subversive group, the church doesn't immediately pop into the mind.

Jesus was a dangerous subversive.

He was a threat to the establishment. He questioned authority. He built his movement on the rabble, the down-trodden, the worst of sinners. No wonder the religious authorities, the scribes and Pharisees, dogged his every step looking for a reason to arrest him.

And what reasons he gave them! He healed on the Sabbath. He ate with prostitutes. He didn't keep the fast. He claimed he could forgive sins. He even threatened to destroy the temple. If we want a modern parallel to Jesus, we should look not to current religious leaders, but to the political radicals of the 1960s and to third world terrorists. To the scribes and Pharisees, Jesus was as much a threat to the social and political order as the Black Panthers, the Weathermen, the Irish Republican Army, or Islamic bombers. If we are offended by such comparisons, it is because we fail to grasp the depth of the Pharisees fear.

True Christianity is revolutionary. It calls us to question the most cherished assumptions of our society and our nation. I sometimes shudder with fear when I think what it would have been like to see Jesus in the flesh. Would I have followed him? Or am I so at home in my world, my country, my religion, that I would have misunderstood and condemned him as a dangerous rebel? What about you?

Are you a Pharisee?

Rule Number One

"Why are you doing what is not lawful?" Luke 6:2b (NRSV)

Barney Fife said it first. In explaining the workings of the Mayberry jail ("The Rock"), he told some dangerous criminals, "We have few rules here. Rule number one is 'Obey the rules.'"

That pretty much summed up the attitude of the Pharisees. After all, what would life be like without rules? Things must be orderly or nothing gets accomplished. Besides, the rules they followed were from God.

Jesus didn't keep the rules.

He was a troublemaker with a bad attitude.

He didn't even keep the most sacred commandment from God: to keep the Sabbath day holy. The Law of God clearly said to do no work on the Sabbath and that was enough for the Pharisees. Their attitude was "God said it, I believe it, that settles it." To intentionally disregard even one law from God was to make him a liar.

But this Jesus worked on the Sabbath. Once when he and his followers were walking through a grain field, they took some of the grain, rubbed it in their hands to remove the husks, and ate it.

Reaping grain on the Sabbath was a clear violation of God's law. Of course, it wasn't the usual way of reaping, but it was work nonetheless. It may seem an insignificant violation to some, but if overlooked it could lead to a wholesale disregard of the Sabbath; Israel would forsake God and face the terror of his wrath. What Jesus allowed was the first step down the slippery slope toward destruction.

"We were hungry," Jesus replied. A weak defense, we Pharisees say, for violating the cornerstone of the covenant. Oh yeah, he also said something about David eating the holy bread in the temple, bread that only the priests were to eat. Of all the nerve! Comparing himself to David. Anyway, our rabbis have shown that David was a peculiar exception to the rule. Why, they aren't sure, but the Lord be praised.

But this Jesus is no David, and his attitude is dangerous. True, God overlooked what David did, but we shouldn't expect him to do the same for us. Better safe than sorry.

At other times, this Jesus healed people on the Sabbath—work beyond a doubt. In defense, he said something about pulling an ox from the ditch. We Pharisees fail to see the parallel.

Jesus is a radical. He even says the Sabbath was made for man, not man for the Sabbath. Imagine! Making God and his law fit human standards. Jesus is clearly a humanist, claiming that people are more important than the law, measuring God by what humans want.

But his ideas can never catch on. It's just too ridiculous to think that people can be oppressed by the Law of God (or our interpretations of the law, as Jesus would say). Anyone can see that it's impossible for God-fearing people to be corrupted by religious power, to forcibly put down opposing views, and to be overzealous in enforcing godly rules. Extremism in the pursuit of holiness is no vice. To think people can be crushed by those trying to enforce God's laws is ludicrous.

Simply ludicrous.

So say we Pharisees.

Hurt Feelings

"Do you know that the Pharisees took offense?" Matthew 15:12b (NRSV)

There is nothing that upsets me more than those times I have unintentionally hurt the feelings of someone I love. Even now it hurts and embarrasses me to think I made them cry. Maybe I was born this way or maybe I learned it in childhood, but the thing I hate most in the world is to think someone is unhappy with me. I'm sure it's a character flaw, for I go out of my way to avoid offending people.

Jesus didn't have that problem.

He didn't exactly enjoy offending, but he didn't let it bother him.

Especially offending the Pharisees.

One time, the Pharisees got on to Jesus because his disciples did not wash properly before meals. Their concern was not hygienic, but religious. There was a certain prescribed way of washing before meals, and if you didn't do it the Pharisaic way, then you were breaking the Law.

Or so they said.

Jesus said, "You've got it all wrong. It's not what goes in to a person that makes him sick, it's what comes out. Don't worry so much about unclean hands, but unclean hearts."

The disciples had no idea of what he meant, but they knew one thing. They knew the faces of the Pharisees changed when they heard Jesus. He made them mad, and you don't want to get in the way of a mad Pharisee.

"Lord," they said, "Weren't you a little rough on the Pharisees? Don't you know you offended them?"

"Oh, you mean the blind guides who lead others into the ditch," said Jesus. "Yes, I know they were offended."

Many of us have known offensive Christians who hurt feeling right and left for no reason. Such is not the way of Christ. On the other hand, we have known those who control the whole church by threatening to be "offended" by every change that is proposed.

My good friend Dale Smith once preached in a small church where every attempt at change was squashed by one good brother who would say, "Brethren, I'm not sure about that; I think it would offend me." Dale proposed a new plan to evangelize the community, the "good brother" objected, and finally Dale could take it no more. "Okay brethren," he said, "you have a choice. If we go with this plan, this good brother will be offended. If we don't, I will be offended. So choose whom you will offend."

The evangelism plan went through.

Dale had learned the lesson of Jesus.

I'm not advocating that we run rough-shod over people's feelings or consciences. That is not the way of Christ. But at times we must overcome our natural timidity and inclination to take the least objectionable path. Sometimes innocent people are oppressed by hypocritical Christian teachers who must be stopped. Sometimes the lost must be saved, the sick healed, and the ignorant taught no matter who is offended. Sometimes the sinner must be confronted, no matter how embarrassing.

There is a thing much worse than offending others. That thing is offending the One who did not always wash correctly.

DAY 11

A Demanding Lord

Matthew 17:24-27; 12:46-50; Mark 10:35-45

"Jesus is Lord," we love to sing. Do we really know what we're saying?

In the ancient world, a lord was a ruler. The greatest lord was the king of the land. This was no democracy. Common people had no rights. The lord had absolute control over you, your family, and your property. He was judge and jury and the Supreme Court in one person. He could (and did) take your sons and daughters for slaves, take your money for taxes, and even take your life if it pleased him. He was an absolute dictator. His word was law.

Jesus is Lord.

Lord of Lords. We may console ourselves with the assurance that he is a benevolent dictator, one who cares for us more than he does for himself. But he is a dictator. He alone rules. We don't even get a vote.

We owe him a greater allegiance than we owe our country. We follow him even if it costs us our family. We follow even though it means going to the cross. Country. Family. Self. They do not rule us. One alone is Lord.

Tax Free!

"Then the children are free. . . ." Matthew 17:26b (NRSV)

In yesterday's mail an envelope arrived saying in bold letters, "Earn Tax-free Income!" It caught my attention because April 15 is drawing near, the date all taxpayers dread. This year, like the last, after all my withholding and deductions I still owe money. Is it worth it? Do I actually receive that much benefit from the Federal government? Even if you are getting a refund, doesn't it gall you to know the government has had use of your money for a year without paying you interest on it? Just try doing the same to them! What a joy it would be if we didn't have to pay taxes.

Jesus didn't have to pay taxes.

Oh sure, the tax collectors thought he did. Even his disciples thought so. When asked if his teacher owed the tax, Peter immediately replies, "Yes." Later, when he saw Jesus, he found it was not that simple.

"Do the kings of the earth take taxes from their children or from others?" Jesus asked Peter. An easy question. Peter replies, "From others." After all, no king would tax his own son or daughter. Princes and princesses owe no tax. "Then," Jesus said, "the children are free."

What's the point? You see, the tax in question was the temple tax. If it is God who demands this tax (as the Jewish tax collectors said), then surely he does not demand it of his Son, or indeed from any of his children. The children of God are free from taxation. And we are God's children.

Is this the greatest tax shelter of all time? Does this mean we Christians can refuse to have income tax withheld? Can we use Jesus' words to inspire a tax rebellion?

No. For Jesus paid the tax. He didn't owe it, but he paid it. Furthermore, our situation is much different from his. We owe taxes not to the temple but to the government. "Render unto Caesar what is Caesar's," Jesus said. Sorry, but Caesar must be paid.

So if Jesus is not advocating tax revolt, what does this passage say to us? Much. For this is not a lesson about taxes, but about freedom. "The children are free," Jesus says. But in order "not to offend them," he pays the temple tax.

Freedom is a precious word to all humanity, but it is particularly dear to Americans. After all, it was the desire for freedom from taxation that motivated our Revolution. Remember the Boston Tea Party and "no taxation without representation"? Even today there is no more sacred virtue in America than freedom, freedom to be, to do, to say anything one desires. Any barrier in our society to freedom of thought or expression is decried as censorship and quickly condemned.

In Jesus and the church we find a barrier to our freedom, a barrier that does not destroy our concept of freedom, but actually enriches it. That barrier is love. As Christians we are absolutely free children of God. "All things are lawful" to us (1 Corinthians 6:12, NRSV). Yet this freedom must not always be exercised, for something stands above it: the call of love.

Since Jesus is our Lord, not Caesar or America, we must place his will above our thirst for freedom. As Christians, it is not freedom, but love that should motivate our actions. Christ came to set us free. Free to love. The church is not like the world. It is not a community of rights and freedoms, but a community of love. When we are tempted in the church to insist on our rights, even on our freedom in Christ, we must remember our Lord who restricted his freedom out of love for us.

He even paid taxes he did not owe.

Focus on the Family

"Who is my mother, and who are my brothers?" Matthew 12:48

We might not be tempted to put our country before Jesus. We might not even be tempted to put the freedom we hold so dear before him. However, in our society, there is one thing that has become sacrosanct. There is one thing we are tempted to place above all others. The family.

My family is important to me.

Family was important to Jesus.

He was part of a family—an obedient son and loving brother. Though single himself, he approved of marriage, creating wine at the wedding feast, and even comparing the coming kingdom of God to a wedding banquet. Unlike many of his contemporaries, Jesus taught marriage was for life. It was he who gave us that beautiful line in the marriage ceremony: "What God has joined together, let no one separate" (Matthew 19:6). Jesus had no children, but he loved children and expected even evil parents to give good things to their children.

Jesus came to destroy the family.

That's what he said: "For I have come to set a man against his father, and a daughter against her mother, and a daughter-in-law against her mother-in-law; and one's foes will be members of one's own household" (Matthew 10:35).

Jesus came to make us hate our family: "Whoever comes to me and does not hate father and mother, wife and children, brothers and sisters, yes, and even life itself, cannot be my disciple" (Luke 14:26).

These are shocking words, words we try to explain away. Surely Jesus does not mean we should actually hate our families. This must be hyperbole. After all, he is the Prince of peace and the Lord of love.

But these are his words. We must take them seriously. Here Jesus is speaking, not of the attitude of hate, but the results of hate. We certainly are not to hate our family members and seek to do them harm. To do so is not to be like Jesus. But following Jesus may turn our families against us. Discipleship may splinter our families, turning their love to hatred. If this sounds far-fetched, remember that many of the early Christians were denounced to the authorities by their own families. Fathers, mothers, sisters, and brothers really did turn their own relatives over to persecution and death. In some places today it still happens.

But what can this mean to us who live in a country where Christianity is respectable? First, it means Jesus did not come to save the American family, he came to save all humanity. Even in our time a truly dedicated Christian may do more than rub her family the wrong way. Discipleship can still cost us the respect and affection of our family and friends.

Jesus wants us to be good fathers, mothers, brothers, sisters, and children. The family is important to him. But the family is not ultimate. It is not our Lord. He is. On one occasion, Jesus was told his mother and brothers wished to see him. His response: "'Who is my mother and who are my brothers?' And pointing to his disciples, he said, 'Here are my mother and my brothers! For whoever does the will of my Father in heaven is my brother and sister and mother'" (Matthew 12:48-49). Jesus came to start a new family, the family of God. It is the Father of that family who demands our ultimate allegiance, no matter what the cost. And it will cost. It may even cost us our family.

What's in It for Me?

". . . we want you to do for us whatever we ask of you." Mark 10:35b

Going to Jerusalem. Was there ever a greater thrill for a true Israelite? Going to the temple, ascending the holy hill, marching to Zion, attending the great feast.

And this was to be no ordinary Passover, for the disciples were on the march with Jesus. At last it looked like he would reveal himself as

Messiah, cast out the Romans, and sit on David's throne in glory. And the disciples would be there with him. What an exciting journey!

Yet their excitement was tempered by some disturbing statements from Jesus: "The Son of Man will be delivered to the Gentiles; they will mock him and spit upon him, and flog him, and kill him; and after three days he will rise again" (Mark 10:33-34). Who was this "Son of Man?" Surely Jesus wasn't talking about himself. He was the Messiah who was leading them into his glorious kingdom.

So thought the disciples. But they did not understand. They were perplexed and filled with a vague sense of dread. Yet even those feelings could not overcome the thrill of marching to Zion with the Messiah. Jesus was king. They were his closest advisors. Power and honor awaited them.

So James and John saw the perfect opportunity to make their move. Beating the other disciples to the punch, they approached Jesus and asked, "Let us sit one at your right hand and one at your left, in your glory." Second in command to the Messiah—what a glorious position it would be!

But Jesus had some conditions. "Can you drink the cup I drink and be baptized with the baptism I must undergo?" "Sounds easy enough," they must have thought; "drink a cup, be baptized, we can do that." They quickly said to Jesus, "We are able."

They completely misunderstood. The cup was the cup of suffering. The baptism was a baptism of pain. But even though they hadn't a clue about what Jesus was saying, by the grace of God they spoke the truth. James, John, and the other disciples would indeed share the sufferings of Christ. For his name they would imprisoned, beaten, and killed. They would learn the hard way that the road to Jerusalem always goes through the cross. Suffering always precedes glory.

We may condemn James and John for their pride or smirk at their naiveté, but are we any better? Why do we follow Jesus? Is it because we expect our needs to be met? Don't we also want recognition, praise, and glory for our discipleship?

Jesus promises glory to his disciples. But that glory comes only after suffering. The road to Zion is not a road to glory, but a path of suffering service. Only after the cross is Jesus glorified. Only after we share his cup will we share his glory. If we go to church to have our needs met, we have missed the point just like James and John. We go to church and live each moment to serve our God and other people. Only the path of faithful service leads to resurrection and glory.

And so the question comes. If Jesus is our Lord, what are we willing to give up for him? Freedom, our most treasured heritage? Our family, those we love the most? Our highest ambitions and aspirations? What exactly does he want from us?

He demands them all. All that we are. All that we have. He alone is Lord. No other.

But he gives more than he demands. Forgiveness. Salvation. New life. He alone grants true freedom. He makes us part of a new family, his church. He promises glory beyond our wildest imaginations. He gives blessing upon blessing.

What begins as suffering ends as song. And so we sing with the psalmist: "Give thanks to the Lord, for he is good; his love endures forever" (Psalm 107:1). The demanding Lord is the Lord of love. We give only what his love has already given.

DAY 12

Strange Companions

Matthew 9:9-13; Luke 6:12-16; 9:57-62

We are judged by our companions. If we spend our time with devout Christians, most will assume we are Christians too. On the other hand, if we associate frequently with those who have no time for God, then many will assume we also have no faith.

Jesus had strange companions. He seldom associated with the type of person we would expect to be his friend. Who would we nominate to be a friend of Jesus? Kings perhaps? After all, Jesus was the true King of the Jews. He was the ruler of the universe. He was Lord of lords. But except for his birth, when the magi bowed before him with their kingly gifts, and his trial, when he appeared before Herod, Jesus had little to do with kings.

Perhaps we expect Jesus to make friends with the religious leaders of his day. The scribes spent their days copying the Word of God. Surely he'd feel at home with them. The priests served God in the holy temple. They would make perfect companions for Jesus, wouldn't they? The Pharisees made it their life work to be faithful to the Law of God. Surely Jesus the Son of God would find them kindred spirits.

It didn't happen. At twelve Jesus is in the temple talking with the priests and impressing them with his questions. Later, they turn against him and plot his death. Jesus eats with scribes and Pharisees, but calls them hypocrites and whitewashed tombs.

Jesus didn't get along with the powerful people. He wasn't close to the religious leaders of his day. He had his values all wrong. He preferred to associate with the powerless who could do him no favors, with the notorious sinners, tax collectors, prostitutes, and others with unsavory reputations. He even chose his closest companions from the ranks of uneducated fishermen, hated Roman sympathizers, and patriotic rebels. He made his home with the homeless. He touched the leper no one would touch.

Jesus didn't know how to pick good companions. His values were all wrong. Which is to say, our values are all wrong. If we choose our friends on the basis of what they can do for us, we're not following Jesus. If we associate only with fellow believers, we do not follow the "friend of sinners." If we are always with the well, we cannot imitate the great Physician.

As we look at Jesus' companions, we will be surprised, but perhaps we will learn more of what it really means to follow him.

A Motley Crew

"When morning came, he called his disciples to him and chose twelve of them, whom he also designated apostles." Luke 6:13

Jesus was about to make one of the most important decisions of his life; he was about to choose twelve special disciples to be his constant companions. He would teach them what others could not hear and would give them power from on high. Then when all was fulfilled, he would send them on a mission of utmost importance. That's why he called them apostles: "the sent-out ones." They would be the pillars of the church. He had to pick the right men.

Jesus didn't even hold interviews.

He didn't ask for resumes or references. He didn't even go after the right people: the priests, the politically powerful members of the Sanhedrin, the scholarly scribes, and the religious Pharisees. In short, he did none of the things we would do in choosing leaders for our country, our business, or our church.

So it's no wonder he ended up with a strange collection of characters as his apostles. Four were fishermen, muscle-bound dolts strong enough to haul a net, but not known for their trained intellects. One was a tax collector, a traitor to his own country. Wasn't the Messiah supposed to rid the land of the pagan infidels? Then why did he pick Matthew, an opportunist who collected taxes from his own people to give to the hated Romans? Another apostle was Simon, a fiery patriot, a zealot ready to defend the Law by overthrowing the Roman invaders. How could Jesus pick both Simon and Matthew? How could he ever expect them to get along?

The rest of the apostles were no better. All were common men, uneducated, with no political power and no proven leadership ability. One would even betray him. Yes, Jesus picked Judas too, picked the one who would sell him out for thirty pieces of silver. He picked the one who would lead him to the cross.

Jesus really knew how to pick them.

Really, he knew how. For this motley crew of common men were to be transformed by the teaching of Jesus and the power of the Spirit. These uneducated tongue-tied laborers would later astound the authorities with their bold speech about Jesus. These cowards who ran at Jesus' arrest would later faithfully suffer torture, imprisonment, and death for his name. These dunderheads who hardly ever understood Jesus' teachings would later be teachers to the whole church, both in their day and through their writings for ages to come.

Jesus knew how to pick them. He didn't ask for interviews and resumes, but he did ask for an all-important reference. Before he picked the twelve, he spent the night in prayer with his Father. It was God who aided Jesus in this important decision. It was God whose power made the decision right.

How do we pick leaders for the church? Do we rely on the best of worldly wisdom? Do we judge by human standards? Do we seek those who are respected, powerful, and successful in this world? Or do we, like Jesus, judge by a different yardstick? Resumes and references may be useful, but in the church, leadership must be judged by the ultimate referee. We dare not chose leaders or make any decision without doing what Jesus did—go to God in prayer.

The Wrong Crowd

"Why does your teacher eat with tax collectors and sinners?" Matthew 9:11b

When I was a teenager, I heard many lectures about running with the wrong crowd. Conventional wisdom and Scripture mixed well at my house: "One bad apple can spoil the whole bunch," "Evil companions corrupt good morals," and particularly, "You don't want to get a bad reputation."

Jesus had a terrible reputation.

He obviously had not listened to his parents' lectures on evil companions. Instead he insisted on being at all the wrong places with all the wrong people. He didn't just try to convert them from a distance, he mixed with them socially. They invited him to dinner and he accepted.

These were no ordinary sinners, but the worst of the worst. Tax collectors who cheated their own countrymen to raise money for the hated Romans. Prostitutes, daughters of Israel, heirs of the covenant who sank so low they would sell their bodies to any man, Jew or Gentile, who came along. These were Jesus' companions and friends.

When the Pharisees called him on it, Jesus replied, "The well don't need a doctor, the sick do." To the Pharisees it must have seemed a lame rejoinder, but to Jesus these words struck at the heart of his ministry. He alone was sinless—whom could he eat with if not with sinners? Like a doctor who risks infection by treating the terminally ill, he risked his all to save sinners, to save you and me.

So whom do we listen to, our parents or Jesus? Not all our fellow Christians will understand if we befriend sinners. Some will condemn us for running with the wrong crowd and accuse us of worldliness. Like Jesus, our reputation may suffer. But we must not withdraw into the safety of the spiritually healthy. We must risk all to bring the terminal sinners to the only one who can cure.

Homeless

". . . the Son of Man has no place to lay his head." Luke 9:58b

We are constantly surrounded by those in need. Most of the time, however, we manage to ignore them by remaining isolated in our homes, cars, and places of business. The sick are confined to the hospital, the mentally ill to a sanitarium, the poor to certain sections of town, and those who are not confined become non-persons to us. We walk down the street and avoid the gaze of panhandlers because we know they want something from us. Perhaps even something more than money.

It was the same in Jesus day. The poor were confined to their hovels, the lepers to their colonies, the beggars to their street corners where they could be safely ignored.

But Jesus broke through the barriers.

He shocked the people of his time, particularly the religious, churchy people, by reaching out in compassion to those others avoided and ignored. His contemporaries could not understand this. Didn't he know he couldn't really help that kind of people? Didn't he know they would demand more from him than he was able to give? That they would inconvenience him and cramp his lifestyle?

Indeed he did. And it did not stop him or even slow him from showing compassion. As we reflect on these stories of Jesus and his love, let us ask ourselves three questions:

Are we not in as sad shape spiritually, emotionally, and perhaps even physically as these unfortunate ones that Jesus touched?

Has he not touched us with his compassion?

If so, how can we ignore those around us who need his love and ours?

It's hard for me to imagine the life of the homeless. Through no fault of my own, I've always had a nice house, a warm meal, and a loving family to come home to. What would it be like to be in constant fear of your companions? To wonder where your next meal is coming from? To face each night the question, "Where will I sleep? How can I stay warm?"

Jesus was homeless.

He actually did not know where he would sleep each night. He was worse off than even the wild animals. "Foxes have holes, and birds of the air have nests; but the Son of Man has nowhere to lay his head." Jesus knew the feeling of being alone, of having no place to call his own. He could look the homeless in the eyes and honestly say, "I understand."

All Christians are homeless.

That may seem ludicrous when one looks at the large modern homes most American Christians own. But in spite of our houses, our wealth, and our prominent places in the community, Jesus calls us to be homeless. "My disciples are not of this world," he says. One hymn says, "This world is not my home, I'm just a passing through." The amazing thing is that most of us can sing it with a straight face.

We are very much at home in the world. We run the world's businesses, enjoy the world's pleasures, and seek the world's glory.

By contrast, the homeless are outsiders. They are powerless in our society. They have no worldly ambition but to survive. As Christians we too are called to stand outside society, to give up worldly power. But unlike the homeless, we do this not out of desperation or despair, but because we have a greater home. Homeless here, we look for better shelter, a heavenly city where at last we may lay our heads down in peace.

Our homeless state as Christians should move us to compassion for those who are on the streets. But Jesus' words also serve as a warning to all would-be followers who expect his path to be easy. No matter what the TV commercials tell you, you cannot have it all. Some of us who are rich young rulers (he was the original "babyboomer") may have to sell what we have and give to the poor, in order to have a home with God. To follow Christ is to renounce all, even our comfortable houses and comfortable lives. It means we live for others, not ourselves. It means we find no rest until we find rest in him.

DAY
13

"Please Leave"

Luke 8:26-39

"Then all the people . . . asked Jesus to leave them. . . ." Luke 8:37a

Evil. Do we really believe in evil anymore?

A recent poll in a news magazine says many Americans today have little concept of shame. Murderers sit in courtrooms facing the families of their victims without a shred of remorse. Guilt? Our therapeutic culture tells us that guilt is only in our own mind, the result of psychological repression. Sin? It's an outmoded word. Who really sees himself as a vile sinner anymore? Isaac Watts asked, "Would He devote that sacred head for such a worm as I?" Modern hymnbooks have changed that to "such a one as I." We don't think we're worms. It's not good for our self-esteem.

Evil—Then and Now

Jesus confronted evil. Real evil. Evil that made its presence clearly known.

He came to the region of the Gerasenes and was met by a demon-possessed man. The man was out-of-control, living naked among the tombs, an outcast from society. For a while his friends in town had tried to help this man control the evil spirit. When the demon seized him, his neighbors chained him hand and foot and kept him under guard to prevent him from hurting himself and others. It did no good. He broke the chains, fled the town, and went out to live alone. No power could tame this demon.

What are we to make of this talk of demons and evil spirits? To many this sounds like primitive superstition. Early humans didn't know about seizures or psychological problems, so they explained them in terms of demons, much as they explained lightning as bolts thrown by the gods. Jesus simply accommodated himself to the times in which he lived. Like us, he knew there was no such thing as a demon.

But it's not so easy to explain away the New Testament teaching on demons. These demons talk, they cry out, they make requests. Later in this story, they are sent into pigs. Did the pigs have psychological problems? I don't think so. As much as we may hate to admit it, Jesus confronted real demons, evil spirits.

What does this mean for us today? Do demons still possess people or did that happen only in New Testament times? I'm not sure. There are stories even today of demon possession. Are they true? I can't say. What I do know is that the world is a strange and complicated place and there are more things in heaven and earth than are dreamed of in our philosophy. I also know there is evil in the world. Real, unexplained evil.

Evil is the only explanation for Jeffrey Dahmer. All his acquaintances in Milwaukee thought Jeffrey was a mild-mannered young man. He wouldn't hurt a fly. But he did. He quietly waylaid seventeen people, tortured them to death, and dismembered their bodies. He even practiced cannibalism. Dahmer's true story is so horrific that the most graphic movie murderer seems tamed by comparison. Dahmer's acts were not fiction. They were real.

How do we explain someone like Jeffrey Dahmer? Is it merely bad chemistry that determined his behavior? Was he just socially maladjusted? Or is there evil, palpable evil, that sometimes overcomes us? When we think of demons, of some supernatural power of evil, we find it hard to get the Hollywood version of possession out of our minds. We remember those horror movies of people with their heads tuning backwards and their bodies floating off the ground. Such pictures are more laughable than horrible.

However, evil is real and it carries with it real horror. I don't have all the answers about demons. I do know that demons were real in Jesus' day. I know evil is still with us. The fate of the demon possessed man is a story for our time.

"Leave Me Alone"

Jesus gets off the boat and immediately confronts this man with the demon. Or rather demons, for later we find many demons had gone into him, so many that the man called himself "Legion." A legion in the Roman army consisted of 4,000 to 6,000 soldiers. Perhaps it's not meant literally here, but even so, the man had a bunch of demons.

The demons recognize Jesus. They always do. They always recognize one who is good, one who has power over them. So the demons cry out to Jesus and say what evil always says to good, "What do you want with me, Jesus, Son of the Most High God?" (Luke 8:28). All evil ever asks good is "Leave me alone."

Jesus wouldn't let evil alone. He wouldn't let this poor man alone. He loved him too much. So Jesus commands the demons to depart. "Why do you torture us?" they cry. When good confronts evil, evil may not see it as a blessing. When we try to help those in sin, it may take tough love. They may even see us not as helpers, but as torturers.

Have you ever tried to help someone who scorned your help? I know some teachers who did everything they could to help a student.

They helped him find a place to stay, got him a scholarship to school, bought him eyeglasses, tutored him without cost, loaned him money, bailed him out of jail. What did he do? He condemned them in front of anyone who'd listen to them, accusing them of exploiting him. Those we help may see us as meddlers. They may think we mean them harm, not good. Jesus knew what that was like. He still wouldn't leave those in need alone.

Back to the story of Jeffrey Dahmer. He was found guilty of his crimes, sentenced to several consecutive life sentences, and sent to prison. At that point the good people of Milwaukee and America breathed a sigh of relief. The monster was behind bars. The evil one was chained. Most Americans forgot Dahmer.

One woman would not. Mary Mott lived in Virginia, far away from Milwaukee. She'd never heard of Dahmer until she saw him on the news. Mary is a Christian who lives her faith. She heard the story of this terrible man and thought, "If anyone needs Jesus, Jeffrey Dahmer does." She not only thought it, she did something about it. She sent him a correspondence course on the Bible and salvation. She wouldn't let him alone.

Jesus will not let the demons alone. He commands them to depart.

And so this man who had no control of his life, who was out of his mind, who ran naked through the tombs, is now sitting at the feet of Jesus. Clothed. In his right mind. His life returned to him, returned by One more powerful than thousands of demons.

Evil is real. Satan "prowls around like a roaring lion looking for someone to devour" (I Peter 5:8). He is assisted by his angels, the demons. He is the Prince of this present world. But the good news is "the one who is in you is greater than the one who is in the world" (1 John 4:4). We do not fear Satan or demons or evil of any kind. Why? Because they do not exist? No, they are real, as real to us as they were to this man. No, we do not fear them because Jesus has power over them. He is not a good man who does nothing. He is the Son of the Most High who has compassion on us and casts evil out of our lives.

This man with the demons was lost. Lost in every sense of the word. He'd lost his mind. He'd lost control of himself. He'd lost contact with others. He'd lost his very humanity. Jesus finds him. Jesus casts out evil. Jesus gives him back his mind. When we are in our right mind we find ourselves where this man was found: at the feet of Jesus.

Jeffrey Dahmer was lost. Lost in every sense of the word. But through the correspondence course he received from Mary Mott, Jeffrey saw one who had power over evil. For the first time, he saw Jesus. Jeffrey came to faith in prison and was baptized into Jesus. After his baptism, he studied the Bible to learn more of his Lord. He too was found in his right mind, seated at Jesus' feet.

Leave Us Alone

The townspeople hear of this great miracle and have to go see for themselves. They come out to Jesus and find the man clothed, in his right mind, at the feet of Jesus. What do they do? Do they shout and rejoice because God has healed this man? Do they embrace him as one who was lost but now is found? Do they fall at Jesus' feet and ask for mercy? Do they beg Jesus to come to their village and teach?

None of the above. They beg Jesus not to come but to go. They all ask him to leave the area. Why? Luke says they saw the man clothed and in his right mind, and they were afraid and asked Jesus to leave.

Afraid? What were they afraid of? Afraid Jesus would kill more pigs? I don't think so. They saw this man with evil that no one could chain. Now the evil was gone. Jesus had power over demons. He had the power of goodness, of holiness. They saw the power. It scared them.

There is a word that contains both "power" and "goodness." A word our world has largely forgotten. That word is "holiness." The modern world has done more than empty holiness of its meaning; it has turned its meaning upside down. If someone at work calls you "holy," you can be sure it is not a compliment. To most folk it means hypocrite, egotist, "holier than thou."

It was not always so. Holiness is a powerful word, a biblical word we need to recover. It carries with it both the idea of moral goodness and the idea of dangerous power. In the Old Testament, the holiness of God was nothing to be trifled with. Moses is told to take off his shoes because he was on holy ground. When Israel reaches Sinai, they are warned not to get too close to the holy mountain. To do so meant sudden death.

Holiness is frightening. Near my house is a large electrical substation with row after row of transformers. As you approach it, the air begins to crackle, your hair stands on end, and you think to yourself, "This is not exactly a safe place." One doesn't have to read the warning signs on the fence around the plant to know there is danger.

It is much the same way when one approaches the holiness of God. One begins to tremble with fear. This is a God who is all good. We are not. This is a God of absolute power, dangerous power. "Warning!" the sign says, "The Holy One of Israel."

This is why the people see the man at Jesus feet and react with fear. They see the Holy One. They see Jesus who is so good that his holiness drives out the greatest of demons. They see Jesus who is so powerful that his holiness conquers evil. They see Jesus and they know their own evil, their own weakness. They see it and they don't like it. They want Jesus to go away.

So he does. He will not stay in a place or in a heart that does not want him. The demons tell him, "Go away. Leave us alone." He will not go away, but stays and casts them out. The Gerasenes say, "Go away," and he goes. Why? Because there is something worse than demons, worse than evil, worse than sin. What can be worse than being a sinner? Being a sinner who won't admit your sin, who won't allow Jesus to forgive. By seeing his holiness we also see the depth of our sin. We can ignore that sin by sending him away. Without him there to remind us, our shame and guilt don't seem as bad. But they are. They rob us of our minds, our senses, our humanity. They leave us lost among the tombs of contemporary culture. If we send him away, we send away our only hope.

Or our fear of Jesus can move us to fall at his feet. If we embrace his terrible holiness we also find his bottomless mercy. He casts out our demons. He clothes us in robes of righteousness. He saves.

He even saved Jeffrey Dahmer. The end of Dahmer's story is well known. Just a few weeks after he was saved, he is himself the victim of a bloody murder. Some would say he finally got what he deserved, and in terms of justice, they would be right. I believe he got more. He received mercy.

A month or so after Dahmer's death, I received a newsletter from a nationally popular Christian radio program. The newsletter assured its readers that there was something not quite theologically sound with Dahmer's baptism. The tone of the letter suggested that good Christians could rest assured that a horrible murderer like Dahmer had not stained their honorable name. Why would anyone question God's grace to Dahmer?

Fear. Fear that God's grace might really be free, free to the worst of sinners. Fear that Jesus might forgive indiscriminately. Afraid that Jesus' holiness might be smudged by saving such a one.

I believe Jesus has the power to overcome evil. Even the evil of Jeffrey Dahmer. He overcomes, not by ignoring the evil, but by forgiving it. I believe Jeffrey Dahmer is my brother in Christ. I find that greatly assuring. If God saved Dahmer, he can save even me.

Go and Tell

The Gerasenes ask Jesus to leave. As he boards the boat to go, the man he saved begs to go with him. The crowd wants Jesus far away from them. The man wants him near. Jesus agrees to the demons' request. He sends them into the hogs. Jesus agrees to the crowd's request. He leaves their country. He does not grant the man's request. He sends him away.

Why? Why wouldn't Jesus let the man go with him? Why does Jesus say no to this man when he had told so many others, "Follow me?"

Because he has another plan for the man, a higher call. The Gerasenes will not allow Jesus to stay, so Jesus sends this man in his place. "'Return home and tell how much God has done for you.' So the man went away and told all over town how much Jesus had done for him" (Luke 8:39).

We are not among those who say to Jesus, "Please leave." We are those who admit their sin, who turn to him, who know that he alone can cast out evil from our lives.

And he did. On the cross. And he does. By his resurrection. So we sit at his feet, never wanting to leave.

But he bids us go. He wants us to go and tell. There are others around us who need to know what he has done for us. What he can do for them. So we go and tell all over our towns how much he has done for us.

What do you say to Jesus?

"Leave me alone," you say.

He seeks us through long days and nights, but if we insist, he goes his way.

"Let me go with you," you say. He bids you come. Follow. Then go. Tell.

DAY

14

Are You Hungry?

Mark 8:14-21

"Why are you talking about having no bread?" Mark 8:17b

Suddenly it appears on the screen, larger than life. Thick caramel topped with peanuts. Your mouth begins to water. You've ignored your hunger all day. You can ignore it no longer.

Then comes a molten river of chocolate slowly covering the bar from end to end. To top it all is a jingle, "The snack that really satisfies."

I don't even like candy bars, but if I'm hungry enough and the ad is enticing enough, I can't resist.

On television, billboards, radio, and magazines, we see them every day, hundreds of thousands of them in a lifetime: advertisements. They promise to satisfy all our hungers, even our deepest needs. Are you lonely? The right toothpaste, perfume, or deodorant will bring people close. Are you worried about the future? Just grab a piece of the rock and you'll have peace of mind. Kids doing poorly in school? The latest video series will give them straight As. Advertising not only promises to satisfy our old needs, it even creates hunger for new products we never knew we needed. "New and improved" is its motto.

What would starving children from other parts of the world think if they suddenly found themselves in our living rooms? How could they fathom a culture where food is plentiful, but people are never satisfied? How could they understand our "hungers" when their hunger is so pressing? They hunger for food. A little bread will satisfy. It will even save their lives.

Feeding the Hungry

Jesus knew what it was like to be hungry. Really hungry. He felt compassion for the hungry, so he fed them.

On one occasion, Jesus wanted to get away with his disciples. This was to be a retreat for them, a time of rest. The crowd that followed Jesus had other plans. They found out where Jesus was going and beat him there. We know what it's like to need to get away for a while. How wonderful it would be to have a Saturday by ourselves! We also know how irritated we get when people interrupt out time alone.

Jesus is not irritated. He arrives and sees the crowd. Another man might have sent them away. After all, they were interfering with his plans for a quiet getaway. But Jesus had compassion on them, for they struck him as sheep without a shepherd. They needed guidance. They were hungry for direction in their lives.

So Jesus began to teach them what they needed to hear. He teaches long past supper time. The disciples come to Jesus with a suggestion: "Lord, you'd better dismiss the crowd so they can go into the surrounding villages and buy food."

Jesus startles them by saying, "No, you give them something to eat."

"Lord, it would cost eight month's wages to feed this mob! Should we spend all we have on them?"

"How much food do you have?"

"Five loaves and two fish."

"Tell the people to get ready to eat."

We know the story. He blessed the loaves and broke them. The fish also. The people ate and were satisfied. The leftovers filled twelve baskets. Jesus satisfied the hunger of five thousand with five loaves and two fish, with more left over than what he started with. Jesus knew what it was like to be hungry, so he fed the hungry.

An amazing miracle. Particularly amazing because a few days later it happened again. Another crowd gathers to hear Jesus. They follow him for three days and run out of food. Jesus calls his disciples and asks, "What should I do? If I send them home hungry, some will collapse on the way."

What do the disciples say? What would you say? How about, "Lord, why don't you do one of those food miracles like you did a few days ago?"

That's not what the disciples say. They still don't get it. They say, "We're out here in the middle of nowhere. Where can we get enough bread to feed this crowd?"

"How many loaves do you have?" Jesus asks.

"Seven, and a few fish."

"Get the crowd ready to eat."

So Jesus takes the loaves and fish, blesses them, breaks them, and gives them to the crowd. Four thousand people have their hunger satisfied. This time the leftovers fill seven baskets.

Immediately afterward, the Pharisees ask Jesus for a sign from heaven. How big a sign do they want? Isn't feeding nine thousand people with a few loaves enough for them? But the Pharisees don't understand. Neither do the disciples. Jesus knew what it was like to be hungry, so he satisfied the hungry. He would not turn stones to bread for himself, but he would multiply loaves and fish for others. He feeds us too. More than that, he teaches us how to be hungry: hunger for God, not for food. God alone can satisfy.

What Doesn't Satisfy

Jesus alone satisfies. The disciples saw Jesus feed the five thousand, then the four thousand, but they didn't understand the lesson. They still didn't know how to be hungry.

Immediately after the feeding of the four thousand, Jesus and the disciples get into a boat. The disciples forgot to bring bread for the journey, except for one loaf. This is right after the Pharisees had demanded a sign from Jesus.

Jesus warns the disciples, "Beware of the yeast of the Pharisees and Herod."

"Oh, no!" the disciples think. "He knows we forgot the bread. That's why he's talking about yeast."

With their own eyes, the disciples had seen what Jesus could do with a loaf of bread: He could feed a multitude. Now they worry that they might not have enough bread. How stupid could they be? Jesus reminds them of the miracles of the loaves and asks, "Do you still not understand?" (Mark 8:21).

No answer comes.

It's amazing, but they didn't understand.

Do we?

Sure we do. We know Jesus was talking about the teaching of the Pharisees and Herod. He was warning the disciples not to think like them. The Pharisees could see the mighty hand of Jesus in the feeding of the four thousand and still demand a sign. No matter what Jesus did, they were never satisfied. The yeast or bread of the Pharisees was this unbelief. The bread of unbelief can never fill disciples like the bread of Jesus.

Is the bread of the Pharisees still with us today? I'm afraid it is. Some disciples still demand signs from Jesus in spite of how he has fed us in the past. "Yes, Lord," we say, "I know you've taken care of me in the past. I've never been hungry. You've healed me when I'm sick. You've given me family and friends to cheer me. You've filled my every need."

"But what have you done for me lately?"

Isn't this the attitude of the Pharisees who demand a sign? Are we guilty of the same? If you say no, then tell me: If you trust Jesus to provide for you, why do you buy all those things you see on TV?

"That's going too far," you say. "There's nothing wrong with buying toothpaste or deodorant or tennis shoes. We need those things."

We may. The question is not, "Did you buy the products?" but "Did you buy the advertising?" Do you deep down believe that this product, this technique, this "new and improved" thing will bring you a bit more happiness? Do you in any way think it really satisfies? Does it actually make life better?

If so, we (like the Pharisees) are looking for satisfaction in the wrong places. Like them, we are not content with Jesus. We want more.

What Really Satisfies

You cannot have the world and have God too. You cannot rely on physical bread and expect the bread that really satisfies. This is the lesson Jesus learned in the wilderness. There is only one thing that satisfies. One kind of bread brings life: the bread of God. The Word of God.

We Christians, like the disciples, sometimes do not understand. We still live as if the things of this world can make us happy. We still trust our bank accounts instead of the One who turns one loaf into many. One lesson of the feeding miracles: Jesus can give us all the food we need. The greatest lesson: Jesus alone can give us the food that truly satisfies. He feeds not just with bread, but with himself. He satisfies more than physical hunger.

Are you hungry? I know you are. We all have hungers. Deep, true hungers. We hunger for food, for friendship, for understanding, for meaning, for belonging. To be human is to hunger. Jesus knows what it's like to be hungry, so he feeds the hungry. He fills all hungers.

Are we satisfied with Jesus? Or do we hunger for all the other things that promise to satisfy? They promise, but can't deliver. Jesus feeds and we never go hungry.

We are disciples. We follow Jesus. Of course we are satisfied with him. How do we express that satisfaction? We begin by talking back to our televisions. When we see those ads for products that claim to satisfy, we laugh and say, "Who do you think you're fooling? Buying you will make me no happier. Only One satisfies." We talk back to TV. We say no to certain purchases. And we do more. We pass true values on to our children. We learn and then teach by our lives what is of true value. We are hungry. Nothing on earth satisfies. Only the Word of God.

Jesus knows what it is like to be hungry. He teaches us how to be hungry.

Jesus really satisfies.

DAY
15

No Time for Humor

Luke 8:40-42, 51-56

"They laughed at him." Luke 8:51

Funny things happen in church. Things that wouldn't provoke a chuckle elsewhere cause loud laughter in church. Children are sometimes especially funny because they haven't learned that church is a place of serious business.

It was the middle of the sermon in a church I was visiting. The preacher was going on about some Bible doctrine; I don't remember what. My memory of his sermon is fuzzy because he had some serious competition. A two-year-old boy who sat near me drowned out the preacher with his own talking. "Quiet!" his father whispered time after time. It did no good. The boy continued to talk.

Finally, the exasperated father stood up, tucked his son under his arm, and headed toward the back of the church. As he reached the back door, his son shouted in a loud voice, "Ya'll pray for me!"

I'm sure I'm not the only one who forgot the rest of the sermon.

It happens in weddings too. When my sister-in-law Sandy got married, everyone looked elegant. The groom and groomsmen were in tuxedos, the bridesmaid in their beautiful dresses. Sandy was particularly lovely. Standing there with the preacher, they made a picture-perfect Norman Rockwell portrait of nuptial bliss. With one exception. The young ring bearer spent the entire ceremony twirling the satin ring pillow round and round his head.

We could multiply such scenes indefinitely. Funny things happen in church—at worship, in weddings, even at times of fellowship. There is one time at church that is never funny.

There's nothing funny about a funeral.

Nothing Funny

It was the greatest day of my life. I came home from work that day, and my wife, Deb, met me at the door. She'd been to the doctor that day and I was eager to get the news. She threw her arms around me and said, "You're going to be a daddy."

I could do nothing but smile.

Deb and I had waited for years to have children. We'd waited so long that some of our friends and family thought we were kidding when we told them we were expecting. Now it was going to happen. The next few weeks I spent each day in a state somewhere between anticipation and terror. We dreamed and planned for the child that was coming. Finding an old baby bed at a garage sale, we lovingly refinished it and placed it in the nursery. We talked of how long Deb would work. We agreed on a boy's name, but had trouble deciding what to name a girl. Each night I went to bed wondering what kind of father I would be.

There was nothing funny about the worst day of my life.

Deb was going for a routine check-up. We discussed whether I should go with her, but decided there was no need.

I was sitting at home when the phone rang. I couldn't make out the words because Deb was crying so. She gave the phone to the doctor who gave the news. Miscarriage. Our baby was dead.

The next few hours were a blur of second opinions, procedures, doctor's offices, and the hospital. For Deb's sake (and mine), I had to be strong. I kept telling myself, "This isn't happening." But it was.

It was months before Deb slept without waking up in tears in the middle of the night. I cried less often, at least on the outside, but even today, tears still come. Not a day goes by without my thinking of my unborn child.

Many tried to comfort us in our grief. Some were more successful than others. The most comfort came from those who said, "I don't have any idea what you're going through, but we want to know that we love you." The worst comforters were those who acted as if it were no big deal. "It's not as if you lost a real child," they seemed to say. In other words, "Face reality and get over it."

Easier said than done.

They Laughed

There's nothing funny about the death of a child. I can't imagine anything more painful. When the innocent are taken from us, we not only grieve, but we are tempted to doubt the justice of the universe. "Why not me?" we cry, "Why didn't God take me instead of my beautiful little girl?"

The pain is worse if she was an only child. Just ask Jairus. A righteous man, a ruler of the synagogue, yet illness strikes his only child, his beloved twelve-year old daughter.

Jairus is distraught. Beside himself with worry. His only hope is the young teacher from Nazareth. Yet he's not sure Jesus will help him, for Jairus and the other synagogue rulers had run Jesus out of their synagogues for healing on the Sabbath. Now it was different. Now it's his daughter who is at death's door. Jairus doesn't care about Jesus' orthodoxy. He doesn't care if he heals his girl today or on the Sabbath. He just wants his little girl well again.

So he goes to Jesus, falls at his feet, and begs him to come heal her. Jesus holds no grudges. He agrees to come. Hope swells within Jairus. The rabbi will heal her. All would be well.

Suddenly, a servant blocks their path. With tears running down his face he says, "Your daughter is dead; don't trouble the teacher any longer." The blow Jairus feared had fallen. His little girl was gone. All hope was gone.

"Why bother the teacher anymore?" the servant says. In other words, "Accept what's happened and get over it. Don't harbor false hopes." Jairus is ready to accept this advice. He's ready to begin the grieving process by resigning himself to the awful truth. He'll see her no more.

But Jesus won't let that happen. He completely ignores the news that the girl is dead. Instead he tells Jairus, "Don't be afraid; just believe" (Mark 5:36). What is Jesus doing? Is he encouraging this poor man to ignore reality and live in a fool's paradise? Is he saying it is healthy to live in denial? No. Jesus points Jairus to a deeper reality. Things are not what they seem. Do not be afraid of what seems real. Only believe.

So Jesus insists on coming to his house anyway. A great crowd has gathered to mourn. He enters the house and they all—Jesus, Peter, James, John, the girl's parents, and the crowd—stand around her bed. All but Jesus cry, the parents in particular pouring out their grief. Then Jesus says, "She is not dead; she only sleeps."

And They Laughed

What kind of inappropriate joke was this? They all knew she was dead. It was cruel and foolish to suggest otherwise. What would we think of a person who interrupts a funeral by going to the casket, and saying, "I saw her breathing. She's not dead, just asleep?" We'd think it the sickest of jokes. We'd laugh, not out of amusement, but out of ridicule. What was Jesus thinking?

He was thinking that he saw something the others did not see. They saw a dead girl. They saw death as final. Jesus saw a deeper truth.

He sends the crowd from the room. He takes the dead girl by the hand and says gently, "Little girl, get up." She does. He presents her to her astonished parents. So amazed are they that Jesus has to remind them what their little girl needs. "Give her something to eat," he says with a smile.

An astounding, unbelievable miracle. Yet it is not the miracle that surprises us today. We know this story. We know Jesus did miracles. What surprises us is the laughter. How could they have laughed? Didn't they know the power of God? Hadn't the disciples seen the miracles of Jesus? What little faith they had.

Are we any better? Don't we have problems that seem beyond the reach of immediate solution? We all have private demons, habitual sins that we cannot seem to shake. What if Jesus said, "You have no struggles." Would we believe him or would we laugh?

We all have friends and family who wrestle with insurmountable problems: marital difficulties, alcoholism, child abuse, financial worries, depression, and despair. Do we really believe Jesus can solve our problems or do we laugh at such a suggestion?

The truth is Jesus has not promised an immediate solution to all our problems. He didn't promise to raise this girl from the dead. But he did. He had the grace and he had the power. Not even their laughter prevented him.

We dare not laugh. For he holds life in his hand, and he can do the impossible.

Laughing at Death

Jesus said Jairus' daughter was only asleep. "They laughed at him, knowing that she was dead" (Luke 8:52). They laugh at Jesus because they know he's wrong.

He has the last laugh. He told the honest truth. Death is not final. It is only sleep.

The early Christian learned this lesson from Jesus. They too call death sleep.

Paul tells the Corinthians that if death is the end, then everything, even our faith, is useless. We are even worse off than the Old Testament characters who knew nothing of life after death. It is better to ask "Who knows?" about death than to claim to know and find you are deceived.

But we are not deceived. Our faith is not mere wishful thinking. "But Christ has indeed been raised from the dead, the first fruits of those who have fallen asleep. (1 Corinthians 15:20).

Christ is risen! He lives! This is the heart of the Christian faith. This is what we celebrate each Sunday. This we believe. Do you believe? Do you know that Jesus lives, that he triumphed over death? I think any Christian would say, "Yes." We may have our doubts, but in our heart of hearts we know he is alive.

And we know that if he is alive then death is not final. It is only sleep. And one day Jesus will return and bring the sleepers with him. "Brothers, we do not want you to be ignorant about those who fall asleep, or to grieve like the rest of men, who have no hope. We believe that Jesus died and rose again and so we believe that God will bring with Jesus those who have fallen asleep in him" (I Thessalonians 4:13-14).

Jesus teaches us how to laugh at funerals. Not that we literally laugh. That would be cruel to those who grieve. We do laugh inwardly at death itself. We laugh because we know the day is coming when death itself will die (Revelation 20:14). We laugh because our loved ones are not dead. They only sleep. We laugh not because we have gotten over our losses. We may never get over them in this life. We laugh because our loved ones will get over death.

I'll never be able to laugh at the death of my child. Not in this life. But I know the day is coming when my little child will hear the words of Jesus: "My child, get up!"

Then I will laugh.

DAY 16

Two Women, One Story

Luke 8:43-48; 13:10-17

Nobody

"... but no one could heal her." Luke 8:43b

There was a woman whose nagging chronic illness exiled her from those around her. She had a hemorrhage that would not stop. The loss of blood made her weak, unable to do all the things her neighbor's took for granted, but that wasn't the only reason for her isolation. She was a Jew and (according to the Old Testament), as a woman with a discharge of blood, she was "unclean" (Leviticus 15:25-27).

Unclean. The word itself is enough to make one ashamed to be around other people. "She's unclean," they would whisper when they thought she couldn't hear. But she did hear and was ashamed.

It's not only the word that isolated her. The Old Testament law was explicit on what it meant to be unclean. No one was to touch her. Any bed she slept on, any chair she sat in was unclean. If anyone even touched them, they too would be ceremonially unclean and would have to bathe to rid themselves of her curse. What is more, in her day Jewish tradition excluded the unclean from the synagogue. She was never allowed to sing or pray or be comforted by the Scriptures in the company of her neighbors.

Think of her pain, physical and spiritual. How often she must have looked out her window and wished, "If only I could be like them; if only I could be normal for a day, even an hour." Worse than anything was her guilt, for she felt somehow it must be her own fault that she was unclean. Over and over again the question sounded in her head, "Why? Why me? What have I done to deserve this?" No answer came. She suffered like this for days, weeks, and years. Twelve years.

Still, she had hope. She heard of a physician who could help her, so she went to try his cure. It did no good. Then she hears of another who'd had success with her kind of problem. His treatments were painful and expensive. They didn't help. She went to physician after physician, desperate for a cure, until her money ran out.

She found herself still in pain, still weak, still isolated from her neighbors, still having to worship alone. Now, to make things worse, she was in poverty, having spent all she owned on physicians. She spent her days alone in her house, a refugee from society An exile. A nobody. Unclean.

Somebody

Until the day she heard of Jesus. We don't know how she heard about him. Perhaps one of the few friends she had left told her of his marvelous power. Perhaps in one of her infrequent trips to the village square she had overheard talk that this miracle worker was coming to her town.

But how was she to see him? He was not a doctor with office hours. Wherever he went, a crowd pressed against him. She was unclean. She must keep away from crowds. What if she tried to see him and someone recognized her? "Get out of here!" they'd say. "What are you trying to do, make the Master unclean?" If that were to happen, she knew she would die of embarrassment.

But she was desperate. This was her last and only chance to be healed, to be clean, to be a human being again. She'd heard so many stories of the power of this Jesus that she knew he could heal with just a touch. Did he even have to know he had healed her? Couldn't she remain anonymous, just touch him in a crowd, and still be healed?

"It's worth a try," she thought. So she wrapped her veil around her face, left her home, and found the crowd surrounding Jesus. Pushing her way through it, she saw him for the first time. Like all Jewish men, he wore tassels on the end of his robe. Reaching down when no one was looking, she touched one of them.

Suddenly she felt an energy she hadn't felt in years. Her bleeding stopped! The long nightmare of pain and isolation was over! She had rejoined the human race. "Now," she thought, "all I have to do is to slip away unnoticed."

But it was not to be.

"Someone touched me," Jesus said, "I know that power has gone out of me."

In those few words, Jesus said so much. *"Someone* touched me." This woman who had been an exile, a refugee, a nobody, was now a somebody. By touching Jesus, he changed her status forever. She is no longer just a sick nameless woman. To Jesus, she is somebody.

"Someone *touched* me," Jesus said. "You see the people crowding against you," his disciples answered, "and yet you can ask, 'Who touched me?'" (Mark 5:31). The disciples find the question humorous. "Of course someone touched you," they think. But there are different kinds of touches. The jostle of the crowd is not at all the same as the woman's touch. She touched him with her need. Jesus always feels the touch of those in pain.

"I know that power has gone out of me." Power. That is what the woman needed. Power to be healed. Power to be clean. Power to face the world again. Jesus gives her that power. And it costs him something! The power went out of him, it drained him. Jesus never gives without cost to himself. His greatest gift cost his life.

"Somebody touched me," he said. With those few words he destroys the woman's plans. Now she cannot hide. Now she cannot keep silent. She has been found out. All will know that an unclean woman had the audacity to touch the holy Master. But she must own up to what she has done. She must confess. Jesus has left her no choice.

So she comes, trembling with fright and embarrassment. She who for years has lived on the margins of society is now the center of attention. Falling at the feet of Jesus, she tells her story: the bleeding, the pain, the weakness, the isolation, the years of searching, the touch, the power, the healing. What will the Master say to her? Will he rebuke her for her presumption? Chide her for her cowardice? Scold her for her shyness?

He does none of these. He praises her. "Daughter, your faith has healed you. Go in peace" (Luke 8:47). We might look at this poor woman and see a coward, one whose faith is so weak she will not confront Jesus directly with her request, but instead goes literally behind his back. Where we see cowardice and desperation, Jesus sees faith. For twelve years this woman had tried all kinds of cures, all false hopes. But when Jesus comes she has the faith to touch him. And that is faith enough.

"Go in peace," he tells her. The Hebrew word for peace, *shalom*, is more than just "good-bye." *Shalom* or peace is the word for wholeness, for being in harmony with the world, your neighbor, and your God. Jesus gives the woman more than physical relief; he makes her whole. He restores her to fellowship with the human race. Now she is clean. Now she can visit her neighbors, shop in the marketplace, and attend the synagogue. Now her heart is at peace.

Everybody

Her story is our story. How do we come to Jesus? We come with sickness. For many of us, that sickness is minor. For others, their illness is chronic and incurable, much like this woman's. Where do we go when we are sick? We go to doctors, as she did. We should, for many times they can help us. Do we take our illness to Jesus? Perhaps that depends on how bad we feel. I guarantee I took my cedar fever to him as well as to the doctor. And he healed me! No doubt the shot and the medicine the doctor prescribed helped too, but even when we go to the doctor, it is Jesus that heals. Let us not be embarrassed to bring our physical illnesses to him, no matter how trivial or serious. He cares about our health. He cares about us.

Like this woman we also come to Jesus unclean. Oh, we don't believe we are ceremonially unclean as in the Old Testament, but which of us at times has not felt "unclean"? Perhaps sickness makes us feel that way. Our nagging pains and weakness frustrate us because we cannot do what we once did, we cannot be our best. We're irritable, hard to get along with, and it is no wonder that others avoid us. Or at least we think they do. Like this woman, we feel cut off from those around us. No one understands. We are alone.

There are other reasons we feel unclean, reasons that are not our fault. Rape victims feel that way. They are not to blame, but they still feel as if everyone is looking at them. Everyone knows. Everyone condemns. Divorced people feel that way. Even when they have done all they can to keep the marriage together, divorce makes them feel like failures, isolated from their married friends. Even those who are widowed may feel unclean. Now they don't fit in. They're a fifth wheel. Those who used to invite them and their spouses to dinner, now neglect to invite them. They somehow have become invisible. Unclean.

Depression makes one unclean. Each day is a struggle to just get out of bed. One doesn't want to do anything or see anybody. We need someone to talk to, but that's the last thing we want to do. No one understands. We withdraw from those around us, but we believe they withdrew from us. We feel unclean.

Sin makes us unclean. Perhaps none of the situations above result from sin. Maybe they do. Even if we are not sick, or victims, or divorced, or widowed, we feel unclean. We feel guilty. We feel guilty because we are guilty. People may look at us and see exemplary Christians, people who have it all together. We know better. We know our hearts have turned from God. We know we've turned them from compassion to our neighbor. "Sin" may not be a fashionable word in our society. It may smack of low self-esteem, of puritanical repression, of an unenlightened past. But in our heart of hearts we know there is no better word to describe ourselves. We are sinners. Unclean.

So we come to Jesus. Sick. Unclean. Weak. Too weak to help ourselves. We come desperate, having tried all the physicians of body and soul, finding no relief.

Like this woman we may try to come to him secretly. We want his healing but we fear to face him publicly. So we hang around the fringes of the crowd that surrounds him. Perhaps we go to church late and leave early, sitting in the back so no one will notice. We read our Bibles, but we read them alone and tell no one. Finally, out of desperation and faith, we touch him. He heals us.

But he will not leave us alone. He calls us to publicly confess what we have done. Like this woman we tell our story. We were sick, unclean, alone. We touched. He healed. We tell our story not just once but with every moment of every day of our lives. And no matter how shy we are, no matter how weak our faith, with the touch of Jesus it is a faith that makes us whole. To us he also says, "Your faith has saved you; go in peace." To us, as to her, he gives wholeness, restoring us to God and our neighbors.

All this if we only have the faith to touch.

Another Woman

Like this woman we must overcome obstacles to get to Jesus: our hopelessness, our fear, the crowd, whatever it may be that gets in our way. We seek, ask, knock, and we keep on without losing heart. Her story is the story of the effort all must make to come to the one who alone can heal.

But there was another woman. She was much like the first. She had an illness that was chronic. Her back was bent, she could not straighten up. No doubt this malady kept her from doing all she wanted. It isolated her from all around her. People avoided her as something misshapen, a cripple, a freak. Though not technically unclean, she must have felt that way.

And she'd been like this longer than the other woman. Eighteen years! There is no mention of her consulting physicians like the first woman. For her condition no one had a cure. She doesn't expect one.

So she goes to the synagogue as she did every Sabbath, expecting nothing unusual. But the unusual happens. Jesus is there. She does not ask him to heal her. She does not sneak behind him and touch the tassels of his robe. Perhaps she doesn't even pay much attention to this young rabbi from Nazareth.

All that does not matter. What matters is: he sees her. Calling her forward, he says, "Woman you are set free from your infirmity." Then he put his hands on her, and immediately she straightened up and praised God (Luke 13:12-13).

Yes, we seek Jesus. We seek him with all our heart. We push through the crowd to touch him. But let us never forget that he sought us first. He sees. He calls. He touches. He heals.

Two women. One story. Everyone's story. Our story. Most of all, Jesus' story.

The first woman's story: how we come to Jesus. Sick. Weak. Unclean. Trembling. Poor. Captive. Blind. Oppressed. Still we come, to touch and be healed. The second woman's story: it is always Jesus who comes to us. He sees us. He knows our sickness, our pain, our poverty, our oppression. He calls us forward. He touches us. He heals. This is who he is. This is what the Spirit of the Lord anoints him to do.

Two women. One story. No matter what our sickness of body, heart, and soul, he touches, we touch. We feel his power. Trembling we bow before him and tell our story. We tell his story. We praise God. We go in peace.

Now a somebody.

Now whole.

DAY
17

A Terrifying Presence

Mark 6:45-52; 9:42-48; John 2:13-22

Some of my earliest memories are of nightmares. I must have been around three or four. At that point I was an only child, sleeping in my room alone, my parents next door.

I still remember the dream. I was running through the forest. Behind me was the being I feared the most, gaining at every step. I stumbled and he reached his hairy paws down to get me.

"It's the big, bad wolf!" I screamed.

My screams brought my mother. I was sobbing by that time. She dried my tears, turned on the light, and we both searched for the big bad wolf. We even looked under the bed, but he was nowhere to be found. I fell back asleep.

I don't have nightmares very often now, but I do have fears. It's not the big, bad wolf that scares me now. It's presentations I have to make, deadlines I have to keep, bills to pay. Mostly, I'm more afraid for people than afraid of them.

It might seem a great leap from nightmares and fears to Jesus. Surely we could never be afraid of him. But the disciples who knew him best,didn't always recognize him. He scared them sometimes.

Those who crossed Jesus, or rather who crossed his Father, also learned to fear him. Those who reject his grace should be afraid, for he is not only the Savior, he is the righteous judge of all humanity.

Frighteened by Jesus

". . . they all saw him and were terrified." Mark 6:50a

You would have thought by now the disciples would have caught on to Jesus. They had watched him heal the blind, the lame, and the paralyzed. They had heard his amazing teachings. That very day they had seen him take five loaves and two fish and feed the multitude. By now miracles should have been ho hum to them; they should have expected them.

But they didn't.

After feeding the five thousand, Jesus sends the disciples away in a boat to cross the lake. He stays behind. A sudden storm comes up and they strain at the oars to make landfall. This had happened to them before. Then Jesus had been asleep in the boat. They had awakened him and he had stilled the storm. This time was different. This time the disciples are alone. Jesus is nowhere to be seen.

That is, until one of the disciples cries, "Look, what's that figure on the water? It's a ghost!" And they are terrified, more afraid of the ghost than of the storm. Who is this ghastly spirit and what does he want with them? They are flooded with childhood memories of nightmares, of spirits and demons on the lake, of things that go bump in the night.

But a clear, assuring voice rings out across the water, "It is I, do not be afraid." Jesus walks to the boat, gets in, and the storm ceases.

The disciples are utterly astounded. And so are we. We are astounded by the thick-headedness of these disciples. Perhaps we can understand how Jesus' unexpected appearance could startle them and even terrify them. But once they recognize him, once he gets into the boat, why then are they astounded? Did they not see him calm the storm before? Had they not just witnessed the miracle of the loaves and fish? If he could multiply loaves, could he not also walk on the water? How dense can these disciples be? "They did not understand about the loaves, but their hearts were hardened" (Mark 6:52). That's not all they did not understand.

But before we condemn them too harshly, we must ask, "Are we any better?" Why, of course we are. If we had witnessed the miracles of Jesus, we would find it easy to believe. If only we had lived in those times! How wonderful to see the sick healed, the dead raised, the loaves multiplied, the sea crossed. Isn't it a shame we live in a time when Jesus does no miracles.

But wait. Isn't Jesus around today? Didn't he promise to be with us always? Do we believe he has taken some kind of extended vacation in heaven, or do we believe he is alive and well in our world? Have we not seen the mighty acts of Christ? Surely he has answered our prayers, healed our sicknesses, comforted our broken hearts, and calmed our spirits. Like the scribes and Pharisees, we may long to see more spectacular signs, but none will be given. If one is truly a Christian, one can by faith see the healing, feeding hand of the Savior.

If so, why are we sometimes astonished by him? He has heard us in the past, we have witnessed his mighty deeds in our own lives, yet we still stand amazed when the terminally ill recover, the quarreling couple are reconciled, and dead churches spring to life. Should we not expect it? Or do we fail to understand the loaves with which he has feed us in the past?

Jesus startles us. He terrifies us. He astounds us. He appears where we least expect him. We too are often hard-hearted disciples. But even in the midst of our greatest terror, he says, "Fear not, it is I." And he joins us in the boat.

Joy to the World?

"Making a whip of cords, he drove all of them out of the temple. . . ."

John 2:15a (NRSV)

"Joy to the world, the Lord is come," we sometimes sing, but the coming of Jesus was not a joy for everyone. It certainly did not thrill the money changers.

We picture Jesus as holy and harmless, meek and mild. The artwork in most Bibles portrays a soft, warm, smiling Jesus. He looks as though he wouldn't hurt a fly.

He wasn't smiling in the temple that day.

Instead he was violent. He whipped the sheep and cattle, perhaps even the moneychangers, out of the temple. He overturned their tables, scattering coins everywhere. The onlookers were stunned. "What's wrong with this fellow?" they thought, "What's his problem?" But Jesus' disciples thought of the Scripture, "Zeal for your house will consume me" (Psalm 69:9).

We may be uncomfortable with a whip-wielding, violent, zealous Jesus. How can a loving Savior act this way? How can he say, "Love your enemies," and then drive them out with a whip? How can he be so inconsistent?

But the inconsistency is not with Jesus, but with us. The Jesus we like to think of and sing about—the ever smiling, always lenient, sentimental, happy-go-lucky, live-and-let-live Savior—is simply a figment of our imagination. There is a hymn we sometimes sing that calls Jesus "holy and harmless." Holy? Yes. Harmless? Hardly. Oh yes, he would not harm anyone, but when we call someone harmless, we usually are dismissing them as powerless or as a crank. Jesus came to shake people up, not to harmlessly leave them alone. The flesh and blood Jesus was as much Judge as Savior. He condemned as often as he forgave. His coming was a joy, but not to the whole world, only to those who received him.

Is this not what the prophets foretold? Malachi says, "Who can endure the day of his coming, and who can who stand when he appears?" (Malachi 3:2). He comes not with peace, but a sword. He brings fire upon the earth. All who see him quake with fear.

Fear of the Lord is more than a figure of speech. The money changers who saw their money flying in the air and felt the sting of the whip did not merely have a profound respect for Jesus. They feared him. They feared his anger, his unexpected actions, and his judgment.

We too must fear him. If we do not, then we have domesticated Jesus and brought him under our control. But he refuses to stay put. His anger breaks out against us, a righteous anger we know we deserve.

Joy to the world? No. Joy only to those who repent and turn. For those who make God's house a marketplace (and they are still with us), there is no joy, only the sting of the lash, the clatter of the tables, and the wrath of the jealous Lord.

Jesus terrifies. But he does so only to calm the storm, to cleanse the temple, to turn our hearts to God. If we do turn, we see the Jesus of our biblical illustrations, the Jesus of the smiling face. His love removes our terror. "There is no fear in love. But perfect love drives out fear, because fear has to do with punishment. The one who fears is not perfect in love" (1 John 4:18).

To some, to see Jesus is to know fear. That's because they really don't know him. To know Jesus is to know love. To reject him is to face punishment.

No Jesus, know fear.

Know Jesus, no fear.

DAY 18

Least Likely

John 5:1-15

"Send her away, for she keeps crying out after us." Matthew 15:23b

Every church faces the same dilemma. Few days go by without someone visiting or calling the church, looking for financial help. We want to assist as many people as we can, but we have limited resources. How do we decide to give or not to give? As individuals or churches, we must have some criteria we use to determine who is most worthy of our funds. Do we base our generosity on need? How can we tell who is neediest? Do we base it on moral considerations? Do we help those who suffer through no fault of their own but refuse aid to the able-bodied who can work for themselves? Do we base it on attitude? Do we give to the humble supplicant, but turn away the arrogant empty-handed? Worst of all, do we base it on race or gender, giving only to "our own kind"?

Jesus must have faced similar questions. Many in his day were ill, diseased, and disabled. He couldn't touch them all. He didn't heal them all. How did he decide who should be healed? We don't know. It was his sovereign choice. The faith of the sick person had something to do with it. So did their willingness to ask. Even their national origin mattered, as we will see later. But the bottom line is: Jesus healed whomever he willed.

Sometimes he heals those who are the least likely candidates for healing. Let's look at two of them. One surprises us with his pettiness. The other surprises even Jesus with her faith. The amazing thing is that Jesus gave both the help they needed.

No One to Help

He seems like the biggest jerk in the Bible. Perhaps that's a harsh assessment, but it's the way he looks to me. He first appears as an object of pity. For thirty-eight years he had been paralyzed. Imagine. Unable to move. Dependent on others for help. Not able to do anything for yourself.

Each morning, for thirty-eight years, he had drifted out of sleep and for a moment forgotten his problem. If only for a moment, he was in his old life where he could jump, and play, and be like everyone else. Then reality set in. He would wake fully and know that his living nightmare continued. But he wouldn't give up hope, at least not completely, for each day he would nag and beg until his brother or his sister or one of his friends would carry him to the magical pool. There he would sit, waiting for it to happen.

And it did. Perhaps a dozen times in his thirty-eight years the pool's water began to mysteriously move. Each time he would drag himself toward the water, but always too late. Someone always beat him there. They were healed. He was not.

So he gave up hope. Oh, he still went to the pool, but he didn't expect anything to happen. Even if the water moved, he'd never make it in time. There was no one to help him.

Until the day a stranger came by.

"Do you want to be healed?" the stranger said.

"What do you think, stupid?" the paralytic thought. But he said with a sigh, "No one will help me, so someone else always beats me into the water."

"Get up and walk," the stranger said.

It had to be the strangest thing the man had ever heard. "Get up and walk" indeed. Didn't this stranger know that was why he was at the pool in the first place? "Still, it won't hurt to try," he thought.

"Get up and walk," Jesus said.

So he did.

For the first time in thirty-eight years, he stood up. He grabbed his mat and headed for home, not taking the time to thank the stranger or even find out his name.

Then he got in trouble.

"You, there," a man said, "what do you think you're doing?"

"Huh?" said the former paralytic.

"Don't you know it's against the law to carry your mat like that on the Sabbath?"

"But the man told me to."

"What man?"

"The man that healed me. You remember me, don't you? I'm the one at the pool, the one who's been paralyzed for years."

"So, who is this who healed you on the Sabbath and told you to break the law?"

"I don't know."

And so he didn't. Until Jesus found him again in the temple and warned him that there was something worse than paralysis. "Don't sin anymore or something worse may happen to you," Jesus said. So the man learned the name of his healer.

Did he stop and thank Jesus? Did he confess himself a sinner and ask Jesus to forgive? Did he proclaim to others what Christ had done for him? Did he invite him home with him?

No.

What did he do? He told on him! Going back to the Jews who had accused him of breaking the law, the healed man said, "I've got the name of the culprit now, the one who doesn't respect the Sabbath. His name is Jesus."

So they began to persecute Jesus and even tried to kill him.

What an ingrate! What a jerk! We can't imagine such ingratitude. Thirty-eight years without hope, he repays Jesus for his unspeakable gift by shifting the blame to him and endangering his life.

How do we feel about such a man? I for one am encouraged by this jerk. He was the least likely person to be helped by Jesus. He was bitter. He was self-centered. He lacked faith. He didn't know Jesus before or even after he was healed. Jesus healed him anyway.

In our bitterest moments, our most selfish times, our most ungrateful days, Jesus can and does heal us too. We least deserve his power and his forgiveness. Out of his compassion and grace, he still freely gives.

But the healing comes with a warning: "Sin no more." We must not remain as this jerk, repaying Jesus' kindness with indifference and persecution. He has awakened us from the nightmare of our paralysis of sin, and we must learn his name, fall down at his feet in gratitude, and serve him evermore.

An Unexpected Delight

People like the man at the pool must have discouraged Jesus. Here is one who received the kindness of Jesus and repaid him with evil. As Son of God he came to earth to seek and save the lost only to find that few wanted to be found or saved. Some repaid his love with indifference. Some with curses. Some even crucified him.

Still he continued to seek, to save, to heal, to teach.

One day Jesus' classroom was invaded by one who was not even enrolled as a pupil. A Canaanite, and a woman at that, she wanted her daughter healed. Jesus' pupils, the disciples, told him to send her away. She bothered them. So he did, saying "God sent me only to the lost sheep of Israel."

Still she persisted. "Lord, help me!" she cried.

Jesus told her she did not belong. "It is not right to take the children's bread and give it to the dogs."

"Yes, Lord," she said, "but even the dogs eat the crumbs that fall from their master's table."

Jesus was shocked, surprised. He proclaimed her his star pupil. "Woman, you have great faith!" He healed her daughter.

Sometimes those we least expect have the greatest faith. Sometimes the least likely candidate becomes the greatest leader. Like Jesus, we must not be afraid to associate with those on the margins of society. We might just be surprised with an unexpected pleasure, a great faith.

Who Do We Help?

This woman is truly needy. She is unselfish. She asks not for herself, but her daughter. She is persistent, so much so that the disciples get tired of hearing her. She asks humbly, on her knees. She seems the perfect candidate for Jesus' charity.

But she does not qualify. She fails to meet the ethnic requirement for help. She is not of Israel. The disciple's words to her are harsh, "Lord, send her away." Jesus sounds even harsher. He calls her a dog. How could Jesus be so insensitive? Didn't he know he'd hurt her feelings?

Yes, but Jesus cared more for truth than for hurt feelings. He was the Jewish Messiah. While here in the flesh, he was sent only to the house of Israel. Pagans like this woman had no promise of the Messiah's help.

Yet she surprises Jesus by grasping a promise not yet made. Later Paul would proclaim that the Gentiles by faith receive the same promise of the Messiah as the Jews. This woman jumps the gun on that proclamation. No wonder Jesus says, "Woman, great is your faith" (Matthew 15:28).

In contrast, the man at the pool is a Jew. He also is truly needy. But he doesn't even ask Jesus to make him well. He is bitter. He is resentful. Later we find him ungrateful and disloyal to Jesus.

Would we help either one?

Jesus heals them both.

What were Jesus' criteria for helping them? Was it racial? The woman was not a Jew. He heals her anyway. Was it moral? Jesus doesn't ask if they brought illness on themselves because of immorality. Was it the manner in which they ask? The woman is humble. The man is not. He heals both.

So what do these two have in common? Nothing. Nothing except their need. Both needed the power of Jesus. Both receive. The single criterion Jesus uses to determine who receives his healing touch is this: Do they need help?

What does this say about our own giving? If Jesus gives to all, shouldn't we? Like Jesus in the days of his flesh, we can only be one place at a time. Our resources are limited. We can't give to everyone, so we must make hard decisions. We must give wisely.

The good news is we know the One who has unlimited resources, the Great Physician who heals all by his own blood. We cannot give to all, but in our giving we must point to the One who gives without limit. Whenever we give money, time, a kind word, and a helpful hand, we do it in his name. We tell good news: Jesus saves. He takes our efforts, however feeble, and endows them with his grace.

Two people come to Jesus. Both are needy. Neither deserves his help. Still he heals them. He helps them. He helps not because of who they are, but because he is who he is.

People come to us for help. They may not deserve it. Still we help them, not because of who they are, but because of who we are. We are disciples of Christ. We follow the one who went about doing good, who fed and healed and comforted, who saves all. We give because he gave.

We give them Jesus.

DAY 19

Set Free

John 11:1-43

"Unbind him, and let him go." John 11:44b (NRSV)

In thirty years of teaching in high school and college, I've heard many graduation speeches. They all went something like this:

"Now young people, I want you to know today that your whole life lies in front of you. Your opportunities are unlimited. There is nothing you can't accomplish if you have determination. Nothing can limit you or slow you down unless you let it."

There are two problems with such graduation speeches. They're always too long (I gave a much condensed summary) and they're just not true. It's a lie that there are no limitations in life. The older one lives, the more one sees limits.

We are limited by our talents. No one is good at everything. There are things we cannot do no matter how hard we try. I'll never be a center in the NBA no matter how hard I try or how positive my attitude. Why? I'm too short, too slow, too small, and too old. Oh yeah, and I can't hit a jump shot.

We are limited by our timing. If you're not in the right place at the right time, you won't succeed. I'm sure that I am the best qualified person for many exciting and prestigious jobs. Unfortunately, they are not open at the moment.

We are limited by our responsibilities to those around us. To family. Think what we could accomplish if we were not tied down to wife, husband, kids, house, and dog. Our churches limit our opportunities. We can't focus on our own spiritual needs because we have to care for others.

To be human is to be limited. These limits are not all bad, unless we think we have the right to be all we can be at the expense of others.

The Ultimate Limit

An older man is talking with an ambitious high school graduate.

"What are your plans now?"

"I plan to go to college and major in business."

"Then what?"

"Well, after I graduate, I'll go on and get an M.B.A."

"Then what?"

"Then I'll start my own business.

"Then what?"

"I guess I'll get married and have kids, the whole family thing."

"Then what?'

"Who knows? After I make a lot of money I may even go into politics or something."

"Then what?"

"Well, when the kids leave home, I can retire and take it easy."

"Then what?"

"I guess I'll get old."

"Then what?"

"Eventually, I'll die."

"Then What?"

Death is the ultimate limit. It laughs at all our pretensions of unlimited potential. No matter what we accomplish in life, death comes. The question is what comes next?

Death certainly looks final. We hope for life beyond the grave, but that very hope makes us doubt. Perhaps our quest for the afterlife is just wishful thinking. "We shouldn't think this way," we tell ourselves. "Our faith should be stronger." Yet the doubts still come.

We need to understand the view of the afterlife in the Old Testament. God gave Israel no clear word on life after death. They were left to their own experience and speculation. Their experience said death was final. One places the body in the tomb. It stays there. The dead do not return. Death is the end, the great leveler of life. All human accomplishment crumbles into insignificance because of this one fact: all die.

Yet in spite of the Hebrew's ignorance of the afterlife, they were still faithful to their God. This is the most amazing aspect of Old Testament faith. With no fear of eternal punishment or hope of eternal reward, they continued to serve and obey God. Knowing only of this life, they chose to honor the covenant their fathers made with the Lord.

The Resurrection and the Life

This was the world of the disciples, a world where few were sure there was life after death. But Jesus came proclaiming the resurrection, convincing many they would rise again at the last day.

One day he convinced them of much more than that.

Jesus is teaching when he receives word that Lazarus is sick. Instead of rushing to his side, Jesus delays his journey for two days. When he decides to go to Lazarus, he confuses his disciples (as he confused the family of Jairus) by saying, "Lazarus has fallen asleep."

"Then he'll get better," the disciples reply. He then tells them plainly, "Lazarus is dead."

As they approach Bethany, Martha greets Jesus with these words, "Lord, if you had been here, my brother would not have died."

Jesus answers, "Your brother will rise again."

"I know he will rise again in the resurrection at the last day," says Martha.

This is a great confession of faith. In spite of the lack of Old Testament teaching on the afterlife, Martha is sure her brother will live again. She is sure because of Jesus. Her confession is great, but not great enough.

Jesus says to her, "I am the resurrection and the life. He who believes in me will live, even though he dies; and whoever lives and believes in me will never die" (John 11:25-26).

It's an amazing idea that someday we will rise from the dead. As Christians, we believe it. Like Martha, we know it. But Jesus does more than promise a resurrection someday. He is the resurrection. Where Jesus is, there can be no death.

We know that from the rest of the story. Jesus sees the pain of Mary and Martha. He shares that pain. He weeps with them. Some standing there do not believe he really cares. "Could not he who opened the eyes of the blind man have kept this man from dying?" they ask (John 11:37).

Jesus shows his compassion in a way they could not imagine. He goes to the tomb and says, "Roll away the stone." Then, after praying, he commands, "Lazarus, come out!"

And Lazarus comes. Alive.

To Lazarus the answer to "Then what?" was simple. After death, he saw Jesus. The answer is the same for us. After death, resurrection.

Jesus raises Lazarus from the dead as a preview of his own resurrection. I believe with my whole heart that Jesus was raised from the dead. Yet strangely I find it easier to believe in the resurrection of Christ than in my own resurrection. Death seems so much like the end. We don't know what comes beyond. If only someone we trust could return to tell us what it will be like.

One has! His name is Lazarus. Another has. His name is Jesus. His resurrection is not just some old historic fact. His resurrection is our resurrection. He's the first fruits, Paul says, the preview of what will happen to us all. If we believe Jesus was raised from the dead, then we can be sure our mothers, fathers, wives, husbands, and children will be raised. We know the ultimate end of our own death: resurrection, new life.

What keeps us from believing? Our distrust of wishful thinking? We may want so much to believe that death is not the end that our own desire to believe makes us doubt. We know that wishing for something doesn't make it true. Neither does it make it false. If our heart's desire is for life after death, we may get what we want. More than "may," we will, if we shift our focus from our desires to what happened two thousand years ago on a hillside in Judea. The tomb was empty. Lazarus was alive. He ate and drank and spoke. A few days later another tomb would be empty. Resurrection himself came back to life.

What keeps us from believing? Our scientific age? We know that bodies decay; they turn to dust; they are scattered to the four winds. We know people don't come back from the grave. Science proves it. We also know human beings do not walk on water, still storms by their words, or turn one boy's lunch into enough to feed five thousand. But one did. The same God who gave him that power is the God who raised him from the dead. He's the same God who will raise us.

What keeps us from believing? Perhaps more than anything it's our own view of death. Too many funerals, too many graves convince us that death is the end. It is not. Christ is risen. With his resurrection he changed the face of death forever. Death lives on borrowed time. The day will come when death itself will die (Revelation 20:14), when we will live forever with our risen Lord.

> When the perishable has been clothed with the imperishable, and the mortal with immortality, then the saying that is written will come true: "Death has been swallowed up in victory."
>
> "Where, O death, is your victory?
>
> Where, O death, is your sting?"
>
> The sting of death is sin, and the power of sin is the law. But thanks be to God! He gives us the victory through our Lord Jesus Christ. 1 Corinthians 15:54-57

Life Without Limits

We believe that day of resurrection will come. We believe more than that. We believe Jesus when he said he is the resurrection and the life.

What difference does that make in our lives now? The difference is summed up in the words Jesus spoke after he raised Lazarus. Lazarus came from the tomb still bound by his grave clothes. Jesus said, "Unbind him, and let him go."

We live our lives bound, limited, tied up like Lazarus. We are not yet dead, but the fear of death ties our hands and limits all we do. Jesus changes all that. Now he sets us free from death. He unbinds that fear that shrouds our hearts.

To be human is to be limited, but we need not fear the greatest limit of all. For those outside of Christ, death puts an end to all their accomplishments, hopes, and dreams. Not so for us who know Jesus as the resurrection and the life.

Our task is to stand fast, to not be moved. Our doubts will assail us. Stand fast. Our friends will scoff. Stand fast. We will grow tired. Stand fast. Our work will not go unrewarded.

When Jesus raised Lazarus, he raised us too. He showed that he will raise us at the last day. He showed that he has the power to raise us now. He is resurrection. The life we live in him is new life, resurrection life. He is the life. We believe in him and we will never die. Like Lazarus, we will only sleep. Like Lazarus, we hear his voice. Like Lazarus, we feel his hands free us from all that binds.

Even death.

DAY 20

The Problem with Excellence

Mark 9:33-39

"If anyone wants to be first, he must be the very last, and the servant of all." Mark 9:35b

I am worried about excellence. For many years now we have been bombarded with the word "excellence." It began in business circles then trickled down to Christian schools, colleges, and other ministries. Now it is a watchword in many churches.

Who could be alarmed at excellence? What could be wrong with excellence?

Nothing, if one the word simply means giving one's best for God. "Whatever you do, work at it with all your heart, as working for the Lord, not for human masters, since you know that you will receive an inheritance from the Lord as a reward. It is the Lord Christ you are serving" (Colossians 3:23-24). We are called to love God and neighbor with all that we are (Mark 12:29-31). We must always give our best to God and others. If that is what our churches, schools, and others mean by "excellence," then it is surely a biblical idea.

Excellence as Excelling Others

However, in my experience, excellence is more often associated with success. To be excellent means to be bigger. To win. To be recognized as premier.

But that goes directly against the teaching of Jesus.

> They came to Capernaum. When he was in the house, he asked them, "What were you arguing about on the road?" But they kept quiet because on the way they had argued about who was the greatest.
>
> Sitting down, Jesus called the Twelve and said, "Anyone who wants to be first must be the very last, and the servant of all." Mark 9:33-39

Excellence always means excelling, that is, doing better than someone else. It necessarily leads to questions of "Who is the greatest?" The way of Jesus is not the way of being superior to others. It is the way of the servant. It is the counter-cultural way of the cross. In the words of Henri Nouwen:

> The way of the Christian leader is not the way of upward mobility in which our world has invested so much, but the way of downward mobility ending on the cross... Here we touch the most important quality of Christian leadership in the future. It is not a leadership of power and control, but a leadership of powerlessness and humility in which the suffering servant of God, Jesus Christ, is made manifest. "(*In the Name of Jesus*, 62-63)

So our schools, ministries, and churches should not pursue excellence, but servanthood. We should measure ourselves by the standard of Christ, who gave himself on the cross, not by the standards of the world. We do not want to be superior to others. We want to be like Jesus.

Of course, you say, that is why we want to have excellence in our church, for the sake of saving souls. But even then we subtlety desire spiritual success. We want our college or ministry or church to be bigger and better.

When the seventy-two disciples are sent out by Jesus, they have an excellent ministry. Yet Jesus tells them not to measure themselves by results.

> The seventy-two returned with joy and said, "Lord, even the demons submit to us in your name."
>
> He replied, "I saw Satan fall like lightning from heaven. I have given you authority to trample on snakes and scorpions and to overcome all the power of the enemy; nothing will harm you. However, do not rejoice that the spirits submit to you, but rejoice that your names are written in heaven."
>
> Luke 10: 17-20

Excellence as Elitism

More recently, in many Christian university and church circles, I have heard less talk of excellence and more talk of being an "elite" institution. "Elite" appeals to the snob in all of us. Who wants to be ordinary when one can be above the crowd? Why associate with the average or the lowly, when one can walk with kings?

The only problem with that is this: Jesus walked with the lowly. That's what got him in trouble with the elite. Take a look again at the "elite" ministry of Jesus. He welcomed traitors, prostitutes, the sick, and the sinful. They enjoyed being around Jesus and I believe he enjoyed being with them.

True, Jesus also ate with the Pharisees, but those meals always ended with his puncturing their pretense of elitism. True, Jesus encountered governors and kings, but if you remember Herod and Pilate, those elite encounters did not go so well.

And it wasn't just Jesus. The early Christians were not elite.

> Brothers and sisters, think of what you were when you were called. Not many of you were wise by human standards; not many were influential; not many were of noble birth. But God chose the foolish things of the world to shame the wise; God chose the weak things of the world to shame the strong." 1 Corinthians 1:26-27

From Excellence to Faithfulness

So I suggest we take our cues from Jesus and the early church. Let's leave the "excellence" and "elite" language and strive to be faithful servants. Let us not measure ourselves by accomplishments or by others, but simply trust the Spirit to produce his fruit in us. What if we worked hard to be servants, not to be elite? What if our desire was not to be "number one" but to hear the words, "Well done, good and faithful servant" (Matthew 25:21).

What if our goal was fruitfulness, not excellence?

DAY
21

Lost and Found

Luke 15:1-32

When I was three I got lost in a department store.

My mother had just left me for a moment to get something on the next aisle. I was looking at some toys, not really paying attention to her. Suddenly, she was gone. I panicked. Crying, I ran from aisle to aisle, looking for her. Running and looking in the wrong direction. It took her less than a minute to find me, but it seemed like a lifetime. I'll never forget that feeling.

We all know what it's like to be lost. Like most men, I'll never admit I'm lost while driving. "Why don't we stop and ask directions?" my wife will ask. But I have a pat reply: "I've never been lost, at least not so lost I wasn't found. At least, not yet." Unfortunately, the pat reply doesn't get me any nearer my planned destination. I usually end up asking directions, relying on someone else to find me.

There are many ways of being lost. Drugs and alcohol can make you feel lost, disconnected from all around you. To be lonely is to feel lost. We can be lost and alone in the largest of crowds. Even those people who seem to have it all together can be lost. Lost people are not always easy to find, particularly when they don't want to be.

Once the Pharisees and the teachers of the law got on to Jesus for eating with notorious sinners. In reply Jesus told them three stories. Stories about things lost and found.

A Dog and a Sheep

"Then he calls his friends and neighbors together and says, 'Rejoice with me; I have found my lost sheep.'" Luke 15:6

When I was a kid I might have qualified as the world's worst dog owner. My first few experiences with dogs were not happy ones. The first dog we had was a small black mutt with one eye and sharp claws. I'm not sure if it was the way he scratched my legs every time I went out in the yard to play or his grotesque appearance, but for whatever reason, I was afraid of him.

The next dog I remember was so large and vicious we had to keep him chained. Finally one night, he broke his chain, jumped the fence, and went on his merry way.

The dog that finally stuck to our family was a Chihuahua. The ugliest dog on earth. It looked like a large rat. We named her Suzy.

As you can tell, I'm not much of a dog lover. If you are one, you may regret that someone like me was ever allowed to have a dog. But you have to admit, it's awfully hard to warm up to a Chihuahua. It's not that I was cruel to Suzy. I just wasn't that fond of her.

Until the day she got lost.

I went out to feed her and she wasn't in the fenced yard. I looked and called and finally found where she had dug her way out.

I was heart-broken. We all looked for her for days. Finally we gave up.

Then it happened. One day I came home from school and there she was, sitting in her doghouse as if nothing had happened. I hugged her as I never had before. She was lost. Now she was found.

Jesus told the story, not of a lost dog, but a lost sheep. This was no pet, but a means of livelihood. A man was a wealthy shepherd. He had a large flock of a hundred sheep. One day he's counting them going into the sheepfold: "Ninety-seven, ninety-eight, ninety-nine. . . . " No "one hundred." A sheep is lost.

So he goes and searches and finds. He's so happy when he finds it, he hefts it on his shoulders and brings it home. He calls the neighbors. "I've found my sheep." They share his joy.

It seems an insignificant story. But this is no ordinary shepherd. He is not content to cut his losses; one out of a hundred is no big deal. Why leave the ninety-nine? Something might happen to them. But he cannot stand for even one to be lost. He'll do whatever it takes to find it. And he'll carry it gently home on his own broad shoulders.

A Pen and a Coin

"Does she not light a lamp, sweep the house and search carefully until she finds it?" Luke 15:8b

A few months ago I lost my favorite pen. I know for some of you that sounds like no great loss. I could just go out and buy another.

But you don't understand. This was no ordinary pen. It didn't cost that much, but I had used it for years. With it I'd written notes for my classes, outlines for sermons, letters to friends, and even books that have not been (and may never be) published. The pen was a part of me. If that sounds strange then think of your own favorite tool or saucepan or whatever you use daily.

I had to find that pen.

I looked everywhere. In drawers. In pockets. Under beds. In the refrigerator (didn't Sherlock Holmes say something about exhausting all the possibilities, no matter how improbable?). No pen.

Finally I gave up. It was near Christmas by then, so I started dropping hints for a new pen. But a new one would never be the same.

You can guess what happened. A week before Christmas I found my pen. The new one still sits in the box in which it came. The old one is in my pocket.

Jesus moves from a rich shepherd to a poor woman. She has only ten coins. One day she loses one, a tenth of her net worth. It might even be that these were no ordinary coins, but her marriage dowry. If so, it would be like losing her wedding ring. No wonder she looks everywhere, sweeps her whole house, moves every stick of furniture until (hurrah!) she finds it. She calls her friends and neighbors to rejoice. The coin was lost. Now found.

He had a hundred sheep. She had ten coins. Neither felt they had even one to spare.

A Mother and a Father

"So they began to celebrate." Luke 15:24b

This is a story about a mother and her three sons. A true story, though I've changed their names to protect their privacy.

Mable is one of the finest Christian women I know. I first met her when I was twelve and had just lost my own mother. Her warmth and infectious laughter helped me survive my teen years. Later, when I was an adult, she became one of our dearest friends.

Mable has three sons, Bobby, Bill, and Barry. Bobby is my age, we went to school together. He had his rough times, but now is a good husband and father. Barry is the youngest, much younger than Bobby, and I think of him somewhat like my own son. In high school, Barry was all boy, in trouble but nothing serious, but he has turned into a responsible young man.

The problem is Bill. Bill was always in trouble. Alcohol use, rumors of drugs, a failure at marriage, and brushes with the law. That's certainly not the way Mable raised him. She doesn't know what to do about him; he's a grown man, but he's still her son even when he breaks her heart.

Mable hadn't heard from Bill in over two years: no phone call, no letter, no nothing. She wasn't even sure where he lived, or if he was alive.

Then one day, out of the blue, Bobby and Barry came and said, "Mom, we want to find Bill."

"I do too," she said and sent them on their way.

Through various means, some of which Mable didn't want to know, the two boys found Bill living in a small shack about thirty miles away. Mable and the two boys went to see him.

When they arrived, she said, "You boys stay in the car." She went up the walk and knocked on the door. No answer. She knocked harder and louder. Finally, the door was cracked open about an inch and she heard an unfamiliar voice growl, "What do you want?"

"I'm looking for Bill Hines."

"Why do you want him?"

"I'm his mother."

"Oh no!", the voice replied. Then, "He's around back."

Mable started around the house when she noticed the other two boys getting out of the car. "Get back in the car," she said, "I'll go alone."

She turned the corner to see two legs sticking out from under a car.

"Bill," she said.

He came out, his eyes grew wide, and he began to cry as he hugged his mother.

Jesus told a story about a father with two sons.

The older was a responsible partner in his father's business. The youngest was just no good. He took his father's money and went away. No call, no letter, not a postcard. The father didn't know where he lived or even if he was still alive.

Until, one day, the younger son returned. He was changed. A new man. No longer cocky and rebellious.

But the father didn't even notice. His son was alive! So he hugged and kissed him, and gave him new clothes and a ring, and even killed the fatted calf to celebrate.

The Lost and the Found

"But we had to celebrate and be glad, because this brother of yours was dead and is alive again; he was lost and is found." Luke 15:32

What do you think about these stories? Do you rejoice with the shepherd, the woman, the mother and the father? Do you share in the celebration?

Or do you think, as I do sometimes, that life is not that simple. People don't change overnight. Some price must be paid by these youngest sons. Some lesson must be learned. One shouldn't be able to break a mother's or a father's heart with impunity. This last story is usually called "The Prodigal Son." "Prodigal" means wasteful. The son wasted his inheritance. We might think it is the Father who is prodigal. He wastes his forgiveness on a son who is liable to leave him again.

Such is elder brother thinking. Oh, not the thinking of Bobby and Barry—they shared their mother's joy—but the thinking of the prodigal's elder brother. Safe at home, he was shocked by the extent of his father's grace. Are we?

How many times do we refuse to go and look for the lost, for those estranged from God and us? Refuse because it's not our fault they left. Refuse because we did everything for them and they repaid our kindness with sorrow. Refuse because they'll never change. Like the elder brother, we see ourselves as Keepers of the Standards. If the father lets the younger brother come back with no consequences, not even a probation, then what good is it to be a faithful son. If the Father above accepts any sinner who wants to return, what's the use of being good. If we let everybody into the church, it'll be nothing but a bunch of sinners.

Precisely.

And as a bunch of sinners, now saved, our job is not to remodel the sheepfold, but to hunt the lost sheep. We're not to finger the nine coins, but search for the tenth. We are not simply to work hard at home for our Father, but to risk all to seek the lost. That might mean eating with sinners. It might mean giving up our comforts. It will mean great rejoicing.

Perhaps we don't like to use the word "lost" anymore, because it smacks of narrow-mindedness. Some of us grew up in churches where we thought everyone who didn't believe exactly like we did was lost. Now we believe that there are more saved than we once thought. Fine. We might even have gone from one extreme to the other, now thinking that pretty much everyone is saved. But that's not the case. There are people around us every day who are lost. Lost in every sense of the word. They have no idea of what they are doing or where they are going. Life makes no sense to them at all. Slowly sinking in their own despair, they need help to find the way.

I think it's more likely that we don't like the word "lost" because we know deep down we have an obligation to be part of the search party. To seek the lost is inconvenient. We run the risk of being rejected, of being thought of as fanatics. Perhaps we're not convinced that it all will end in rejoicing.

A lost sheep. A lost coin. A lost boy. When we are tempted to keep our churches the way we like them, when we feel more comfortable around other Christians like us, when we just lack the energy to look for the lost, let's remember one thing.

Thank God, our Older Brother came to find us.

DAY
22

The Other Good Samaritan

Luke 17:1-10

"Were not all ten cleansed? Where are the other nine?" Luke 17:17

We all know the story of the Good Samaritan (Luke 10:25-37). For some of us, it's our favorite Bible story. It's so familiar that our culture has "Good Samaritan laws" laws to protect from lawsuits those who stop to help others in need.

Let me remind you of the story.

A certain man went down from Jerusalem to Jericho. Robbers beat him, took all he had, and left him to die. A priest came by, saw him, and passed him by. A Levite did the same. But a Samaritan saw him and had pity on him. Dressing his wounds, he took him to an inn and gave the innkeeper money to care for him. When he left, he said, "If he costs you more, let me know. I'll pay for it."

This familiar story shocked those who first heard it. They were shocked by the depth of the man's compassion, but more shocked by his identity. He was a Samaritan, not a Jew. To Jews, he followed a false religion. He and his whole land was to be avoided by strict

Jews. But it is this Samaritan, not the priest or the Levite, who proves neighbor to the man.

When was the last time you were a good Samaritan?

The Ten

Jesus had to deal with strangers too. One day Jesus he met ten strangers. Lepers. They had a painful disease that disfigured them, cut them off from human contact, and eventually proved fatal. The Jewish historian Josephus said lepers were treated as if they were already dead.

But these "dead" men can talk. They cry out to Jesus from a distance, "Jesus, Master, have pity on us!" (Luke 17:13).

These lepers must have felt abandoned by God. How could this have happened to them? But they are also distant from other humans. Literally they must keep their distance, crying "Unclean, Unclean."

They cry out from a distance. Far away from man and God. Which of us has not at times felt the same? Abandoned by God and by neighbor. Far away from those around us. No one understands. No one really touches us.

So these lepers stand at a distance, but they have the faith to bridge that gap with loud cries. They do not despair. They still have hope. Jesus, the Master, can save. So they cry out for mercy.

And they are heard!

"Go show yourselves to the priests," Jesus commands.

It is a test. A test of their faith. Do they believe in the power of Jesus enough to keep his word? They do. And as they go, the incredible happens: they are cleansed. Their leprosy disappears. They are whole.

The Nine and the One

One of the ten who shouted for healing continues to shout. His cry is now one of praise. Leaping, shouting, praising God, he turns back and runs to Jesus. Throwing himself at his feet, he gives thanks.

Then comes the punch line. Luke tells us, ". . . and he was a Samaritan" (Luke 17:16). A Samaritan! False teacher! Pagan! Unclean! Yet he and he alone returns to give thanks.

"Where are the other nine?" Jesus asks. That's what we'd like to know. How in the world could anyone show such ingratitude? They had been healed of an incurable disease, brought back from the dead, as it were, and they just go on their way, not taking the time to turn and give thanks. And they are Jews! God's chosen people. They should have known better.

Why didn't the nine return? Were they so caught up in the joy of the miracle that they just forgot? Were they too busy? Were they afraid this Jesus might demand some payment for the miracle if they returned? Afraid he might say, "Follow me?"

We're not told why. It remains a mystery. Beside this, all examples of ingratitude pale. We just can't imagine.

Or can we? How often do we fail to turn and praise and thank? Is this not the whole of the Christian life: that at each moment of each day we live lives that say "thank-you" to the One who saved us? This story of the nine and the one strikes at the very heart of Christian faith.

The nine have faith. Faith to cry out for mercy. Faith to obey the Master's command. Faith to be healed from their dread disease. Such faith seems formidable. Would we have as much?

Yet their faith is woefully inadequate. It lacks one thing necessary for saving faith. True faith is thankful.

True faith focuses on what we have received, not on the good we do for God or for others. Yes, we should do good. Why? Not to receive thanks, not to feel good about ourselves, not to earn our salvation, but because the good we do for God and others is our way of saying "thanks" for the unspeakable gift God has given us: the gift of God's Son.

We can learn the wrong lesson from the story of the grateful leper. We might think the lesson is that others should show thanks to us. They should praise us for the good we do. But only One is truly worthy of praise. All our hard work is an inadequate response to the bounty of his gift. Just before the episode of the lepers, Jesus reminds the disciples that they can never earn the praise of God: "So you also, when you have done everything you were told to do, should say, 'We are unworthy servants; we have only done our duty'" (Luke 17:10).

We can never earn God's praise, for we are only doing our duty. We work because God is the Master, we are the slaves. We work to say "thank-you" for the gift we can never repay. We can deserve no thanks in return.

We can never earn his praise, but by his grace he gives it, saying, "Well done, good and faithful servant! You have been faithful with a few things; I will put you in charge of many things. Come and share your Master's happiness!" (Matthew 25:21).

We learn from two Samaritans.

We learn how to receive. Freely.

We learn how to give.

The same way.

DAY 23

Strange Food

John 4:1-42

My wife Deb and I once spent two months in Wales. British food is not that different from American, yet in the middle of all the sameness, there were surprises. They call their food by different names. Salad dressing is salad cream. Fries are chips. Dessert is a sweet. They even eat differently, always holding the fork face downward in the left hand and the knife in the right. It's not easy using a knife to push English peas onto the back of a fork, but somehow they manage to do it. It takes practice, but after a while I even managed to master the rhythm of eating the British way.

I'm sure Jesus ate the food and had the usual table manners of his day. Yet sometimes he could shock others by his diet. In the hands of Jesus, even the most basic foods, water and bread, were strangely filled with new meaning.

All She Wanted Was Water

"Sir, give me this water so that I won't get thirsty. . . ." John 4:15a

"A woman's work is never done."

"Ain't it the truth," she thought. After a long morning of cleaning, cooking, and caring for her significant other ("The lazy bum; I wish he'd get a job."), she had run out of water. There was nothing to do but to put the water jar on her head and make the long trek from the village out to the well.

Along the way, she reflected on her life. What a mess! All because of men. She just couldn't find a man she could please and who pleased her. Boy how she'd tried! Five husbands and now this live-in. Each worse than the last.

Her thoughts were interrupted by her arrival at the well. A man was there. A Jew by the look of him. At least he wouldn't bother her. Jews had nothing to do with Samaritans.

She lowered the pitcher into the well.

"Can I have a drink?" the man said.

"Are you talking to me?" she asked in amazement.

"Yes. Can I have a drink?"

Something was definitely wrong here. Jews avoided Samaritans, literally like the plague, thinking they would make them unclean.

"Well, I guess so, but look, I thought Jews didn't talk to Samaritans, much less drink from the same jar. Aren't you a Jew?"

"If you really knew who I was," he said, "you'd ask me for living water."

"You don't even have a pitcher to draw with," she said, thinking he was making fun of her. "Are you greater than Jacob who dug this well?" she asked with a sneer.

"I have special water. If you drink it, you'll never be thirsty again."

That would be convenient, she thought. She was so tired of work. So tired of life. To have living, running water would at least free her from some drudgery. "Give me this water," she said, "and it will save the trouble of all these trips to the well."

"Okay," Jesus replied. "But first go get your husband."

Oh boy, she thought. Of all the things for him to mention.

"I have no husband," she said. After all it was the truth. No need to tell this stranger her life story.

"You're right. You've had five husbands and are living with a man now who is not one of the five."

How could he know that? Had he been talking to her neighbors? No, that couldn't be it. He must be a prophet. She tried to think of something religious to say. Prophets liked religious questions. Besides, she wanted to avoid more discussion of her marital situation.

"Tell me," she asked him. "Should we worship at Jerusalem like the Jews or on this mountain like our ancestors did?"

He replied, "True worship is not about place, but about spirit and truth. God wants everyone to worship him in spirit and truth"

With that statement, the conversation took a turn. God wants everyone. "God wants me," she thought. If only that were true. If only God wanted her in spite of the way she had ruined her life. But when Messiah comes, isn't he supposed to bring new life?

"We hear Messiah's coming," she said, still trying to keep the conversation away from her marital status.

"He's here. He speaks to you."

And with those words, Jesus changes this woman's life forever.

A chance meeting. An ordinary conversation. A safe topic: water. The kind of thing that happens every day.

Jesus came to seek and save the lost. He begins the conversation. He asks for her help. For water. Somewhere along the line the conversation reverses. He doesn't ask, he gives. Earlier he had turned water to wine. Now he turns water into something even greater. Living water. Not the kind that gives life but has to be replenished, but the Holy Spirit who gives life once for all.

A trip to the well. Just like a thousand other trips. All she wanted was water. She got much more: truth, forgiveness, salvation, eternal life. Her deepest thirst was quenched forever.

We all know someone like this woman at the well. Divorced five times. Living with a man. Trying to look younger, to stay attractive. We've seen women like her, flashing their forced smiles but inwardly empty. What can one do to help such a woman? How can things be put right? Can the hands of the clock be turned back? Can it be as it once was, before the men, before the failure, before the heartbreak? It seems too much to ask. She'd settle for water she didn't have to get herself.

We are this woman at the well. We come to Jesus asking little: drink, food, health, prosperity. We don't know whom we're asking. We can't hide the facts of our lives from him. He offers more than we ask. We want water, he gives the Spirit. We want food, he gives his Body. We want our immediate needs met, he gives a lifelong relationship.

We need to want more.

All They Wanted Was Food

"I have food to eat that you know nothing about." John 4:32

Where were Jesus' disciples during this fateful encounter? They had gone into town to buy food (John 4:8). Now they return and cannot believe their eyes. Rabbi Jesus is talking with a woman! Everyone knew that rabbis were not to talk with women. Women couldn't understand the fine points of the Law; to talk to a woman would only waste her time and distract the rabbi. If only the disciples had known the woman's past. Then they really would be shocked!

But the disciples had learned their lesson. They'd been burned before by questioning Jesus. So no matter how much they wanted to shout, "What in the world are you doing?" they kept their mouths shut.

Finally, the woman went away. Leaving her water jar, running back to the village, out of breath, she called to her neighbors, "There's a man. At the well. A prophet. He knew everything about me. Could this be the Messiah?"

In the meantime, the disciples work up enough courage to say something to Jesus. "You need to keep up your strength, Rabbi. Here, have some of the food we bought in town."

"No thanks," Jesus says, "I've already eaten. I have food you don't know about."

"How can that be?" the disciples say to each other. "Did someone bring him food while we were gone? Is that why he was talking with the woman?"

"My food," Jesus said, "is to do the will of the one who sent me and to finish his work. If you want food, then look. The fields are ready to be reaped. Others planted, but you will eat the crop."

One can imagine the stunned look of the disciples. He had sent them into town for food. Now he says he has his own. And what's all this about sowing and reaping? We're we supposed to have reaped the wheat instead of buying bread?

But Jesus isn't talking about harvesting wheat, but harvesting people. And that harvest comes. The Samaritans in town listen to the woman's testimony. They go out to the well, bring him back to the village, and he stays with them two days, telling them more about living water. Many become believers. They tell the woman, "It's not just your testimony that convinces us. Now we have heard him with our own ears and know he is the Savior of the world" (John 4:42).

The disciples needed to want more. More than the food that temporarily satisfies. Jesus wants them to care more for people than for food. People are hungry for good news, for salvation. That's the kind of food Jesus has, the kind the disciples don't quite understand. The woman leaves her jug behind. She needs it no longer for she has found living water. The disciples leave behind the Bread of Life to buy food that never finally satisfies. Jesus and the woman have sowed the seed among the townspeople. The disciples are to reap. But they don't quite understand.

We are these disciples. We follow Jesus because of what he can do for us. That's quite understandable since he has promised to do so much. He gives living water. The Spirit. Salvation. Love and hope and peace. But there comes a time when we should hunger for more than just what he can do for us. There comes a time when we must hunger to feed others.

Perhaps we are too much like the disciples and not enough like this woman. We are eager to come to Jesus for what he can do for us. Religion is fine if it meets our needs. We'll go to church if we can get something out of it. Helping others is fine if it makes us feel good. We know how to come to Jesus.

We come to Jesus. Sinful. Confused. Weary. He quenches our thirst. We go to others to spread the news. Come. Go. Come and go, the rhythm of obedience. If we come to him, he gives us strange food. Food that others do not understand. The food of obedience To do the will of God. To finish his work of reaping. To come. to go.

DAY 24

I See

John 9:1-41

"One thing I do know. I was blind but now I see!" John 9:25b

Imagine a typical spring day.

You get up early in the morning to see the sun rise. Soon you can make out the shadowy outlines of houses and trees. Suddenly, the sun peeps above the horizon and the world begins to take shape and color. The grass and trees are a riot of shades of green. Flowers of all colors and shapes are in bloom. A squirrel scampers through a tree. Birds sing. A new day begins.

Imagine.

You turn from the window to see the sleepy but still impish face of your son. He grins and asks, "What's for breakfast?" He's soon joined by the most beautiful sight in the world: your daughter's shining smile. A new day has truly begun.

A Great Miracle

Imagine that you've never seen a sunrise or a sunset, a flower, a tree, a squirrel, a bird. What's more, you've never seen the face of your father or mother or husband or wife or children. Imagine being born blind.

One man doesn't have to imagine. He is blind, blind from birth. In his day vocational training for the blind consisted of giving them a bowl and telling them to beg. So he sits in the same spot day after day, begging enough to barely stay alive. After a while, he's not the only one who is blind, for the hundreds who pass him day after day, even those who throw a few coins in his bowl, soon pass by without looking at him, with unseeing eyes as if he were part of the landscape.

Until the day a young rabbi came along.

His disciples saw the blind man and asked the Rabbi, "Who sinned, this man or his parents, that he was born blind?" The disciples cannot see the man. They cannot see him as a fellow human being, but only as the occasion for a theological discussion. Perhaps they were showing off for their Master, trying to prove what profound thoughts they had. But the man was blind, not deaf! What must he have thought to be used as an example of a terrible sinner, so terrible that God cursed him with blindness? But the disciples were blind to his feelings.

The rabbi is different. He sees the man, not a test case for a theological argument, but as one who suffers. He sees an occasion for healing. "Neither this man nor his parents sinned," said Jesus, "but this happened so that the work of God might be displayed in his life." Calling himself "the light of the world," Rabbi Jesus proceeds to bring light to the life of the blind man.

He doesn't heal him with a word or with a touch, as he had done to countless others. Instead, he spits on the ground, makes mud, and puts it on the man's eyes. He says, "Go wash in the pool of Siloam." Why this strange method of healing? I don't know. Perhaps he did it this way to test the man's faith. Perhaps he did it this way because this is how men were healed in Old Testament times. Perhaps the ways of this Rabbi Jesus will always be strange to us. But he puts mud on his eyes and tells him, "Go wash."

The man goes to the pool and washes his eyes and for the first time in his life, he sees. He must have jumped for joy! "So that's what they mean by 'sky.' And that's a tree and a bird and a flower. Why didn't someone tell me the world was so beautiful? Are they all blind? And this, this the most amazing sight of all: my mother's face." In the midst of his joy and celebration, he lost sight of Jesus, the one who healed him.

A Greater Miracle

This was indeed a great miracle, one unheard of. Indeed, the blind man, now seeing, will himself later exclaim, "Nobody has ever heard of opening the eyes of a man born blind" (John 9:32). Even today, if we were to hear of one blinded in an accident who now can see, we might try to explain it away as a psychosomatic cure: There was no physical problem, only a psychological block to sight. But blindness from birth must be physical, not psychological. Its cure is truly a miracle.

A greater miracle is here, or perhaps we should say a greater wonder. For it is truly a wonder, truly unbelievable, that some could witness this miracle, could know that the blind man they had seen for years by the side of the road now had his vision. That they could hear from the man's own lips that it was Jesus who healed him, and still call Jesus a sinner and refuse to believe in him.

Here is a greater blindness than one who is blind from birth. The Pharisees and the man's own parents shut their eyes to what Jesus had done. They blind themselves to who he is.

What makes them so blind? First, they are *blinded by legalism.* This healing took place on the Sabbath. Such healing is "work" according to the Pharisees, and it is against God's law to work on the Sabbath. Jesus thus is a law-breaker and sinner and could not have healed this man. However, the only law Jesus had broken was one the Pharisee's had made up. It was never against God's law to show compassion. But that made no difference to the Pharisees. Don't confuse them with the facts! Never mind the fact that Jesus had given the man his sight. If the Pharisees said it never happened, it never happened.

The blindness of the Pharisees amazes us. How could they deny their own eyes? But are we any better? Do we ever let our laws, our rules, our understanding of what the Bible says or what God can and cannot do get in the way of what we see with our own eyes? Have we ever denied the power of Jesus in the lives of others because they fail to conform to our notions of what it means to be a Christian? I know Christians who look at the work of a Mother Teresa among the lepers of Calcutta and say it's the work of Satan, just because she is Catholic. We don't have to go that far to see the way legalism blinds. We only have to look in our own church. Or in a mirror.

Legalism isn't the only thing that can blind us to the work of Jesus. The blind man's parents were *blinded by fear.* The Pharisees called the parents in and asked them, "Is this your son? Was he born blind? How is it that now he can see?"

"We know he is our son," the parents answered, "and we know he was born blind. But how he can see now, or who opened his eyes, we don't know. Ask him, he is of age; he will speak for himself" (John 19:20-21).

The parents knew Jesus had healed their son, but they intentionally blind themselves to the fact. Why? Because they were afraid the Jewish authorities would put them out of the synagogue.

Have you ever let fear blind you to the work of Jesus? At the office when someone else is being ridiculed for acting like a Christian, do you speak up to defend them? Do you say, "I too am a believer?" Or does the fear of being put outside the circle of your friends cause you to keep silent or say, "Let him speak for himself. It's none of my business."

Have you ever let fear keep you from doing the work of Jesus? Why do we not evangelize? Because we're afraid of being rejected or being thought closed-minded or fanatic? Why don't we help families we know are in trouble? Because we're afraid to get involved? Why don't we help the stranger at the side of the road who begs from us as this blind man did? Fear of strangers? Fear of foolishly throwing our money away? Fear that he might want more than money? He might want a friend.

We are not to be foolish in our faith, but we are to be courageous. Not a day goes by in our culture that we are not frightened into silence like these parents. May God give us courage to confess what we see: that through his Son the lame walk, the deaf hear, the blind see.

Ultimately the Pharisees are *blinded by willful ignorance.* Jesus tells them, "If you were blind, you would not be guilty of sin; but now that you claim you can see, your guilt remains" (John 9:41). Unlike the blind man, their blindness is not from birth. They intentionally made themselves blind to Jesus. They saw the good he did and called it evil. Refusing to believe their own eyes, they are blinder than the blind man ever was, for they blind themselves to the only one who can cure them.

The Greatest Miracle

We may be blind to the power of Jesus in our world and our church. What is worse, we may be blind to his power in our own lives. To be blind from birth is a problem to say the least. But the blind man had another need more severe than his need for sight.

After Jesus healed him, the blind man lost sight of Jesus. The Pharisees command him to denounce Jesus as a sinner. He replied,

"Whether he is a sinner or not, I don't know. One thing I do know. I was blind but now I see!" (John 9:25).

The blind man had never seen Jesus. He wasn't sure who Jesus was. But he did know what Jesus had done for him and he refused to blind himself to the power of Jesus. The Pharisees responded by insulting him, calling him a disciple of Jesus. Finally they gave him the punishment his parent's feared. They threw him out of the synagogue.

So Jesus found him again. Having given him the gift of sight, Jesus now gives him an even greater gift, the gift of faith.

> Jesus heard that they had thrown him out, and when he found him, he said, "Do you believe in the Son of Man?"
>
> "Who is he, sir?" the man asked. "Tell me so that I may believe in him."
>
> Jesus said, "You have now seen him; in fact, he is the one speaking with you."
>
> Then the man said, "Lord I believe," and he worshipped him. John 9:35-38

It was truly a day of miracles and wonders. A wonder that a man born blind should see. A greater wonder that some could see the healing and still be blind to Jesus. But the greatest wonder is that the Son of Man came to save sinners by calling them to faith. The blind man was overjoyed to see grass and trees and flowers and his mother's face. But the greatest thing he saw that day was the face of the one who healed him, the one who came to save.

No one fully understands Jesus. Even we who have served him all the years of our lives must confess that we see him only dimly. But no matter how weak our faith, like the blind man we know one thing for certain.

We were blind.

Now we see.
So we worship him.

DAY 25

Last Words

John 17

When I was twelve years old, my mother fought a valiant battle against cancer. For the last three weeks of her life, she was sent home to be with us. I clearly remember the rhythm of my days. Going to school. Coming home. Talking briefly to mom. Going outside to play. One day as I left her to go outside, she said, "Watch out for Mark" (my younger brother).

Those words stuck with me. For during that night, mom died. They were her last words to me. And although she probably meant something like, "Keep an eye on your five-year-old brother as he plays," I gave those words deeper meaning. She could not be around to care for my baby brother. I'd have to shoulder part of that load for her.

Last words mean a great deal. On the night he was to die, Jesus gave some last words. Now, you know these were not really the last words of Jesus. He is risen! He lives! And he still speaks today through Scripture and through his Spirit. These are not even the last words of Jesus before he died. But they are the longest prayer of Jesus recorded in the Bible. And they are spoken on the night he was betrayed. The night before he faced the cross.

A Prayer for Unity

The most touching of these last words are words he prays for us. Imagine. On the night he faces death, Jesus prays not only for the disciples he had spent three years with, he also prays for us today.

> "I am praying not only for these disciples but also for all who will ever believe in me through their message. I pray that they will all be one, just as you and I are one—as you are in me, Father, and I am in you. And may they be in us so that the world will believe you sent me. I have given them the glory you gave me, so they may be one as we are one. I am in them and you are in me. May they experience such perfect unity that the world will know that you sent me and that you love them as much as you love me." (John 17:20-23)

Last words from Jesus: "Be one."

Do we take those words seriously? Every Christian I know thinks unity is a good idea. But is it a priority? Do we do what Jesus did? Do we pray for it fervently? And if we pray for it, then we must be willing to let God accomplish it through us. These are last words. That means Christian unity is at the center of God's will for us. It means it trumps church as usual. It means unity is a central doctrine of our faith.

Most of all, it means we must do more than think unity a good idea. We must talk about it constantly. We must go beyond talk to visible action.

A Heart Test

But how do you really feel about Christian unity? In speaking on this subject with Christians throughout the world, I find they usually react with one of four statements. See which one fits you.

"Christian unity is fine, but not with *them*!" *Them* being a particular group you disagree with theologically. We can't be united with them because they are too liberal or too conservative or too literal or too loose in their interpretation of the Bible.

Is this a healthy reaction to the prayer of Jesus for unity? I don't think so. It confuses unity with agreement in doctrine. Or to put it differently, it says we can only be unified with Christians like us, those who are "right" in their interpretation of the Bible or on certain religious issues.

But Christian unity is based solely on our relationship to God in Christ. It's like family. You don't get to choose them.

For example, my brothers and I have nothing in common. They drive big trucks and like going to tractor pulls. I prefer a compact car and going to the movies. They work with their hands and can fix anything around the house. I can screw in a light bulb, given enough time and instructions. They work in factories and out-of-doors. I sit in an office and grade papers. They like to fish and hunt. I read books.

We have nothing in common.

And yet, of course, we do. We have a collection of shared experiences. When we get together we share stories of times in the past. Memories. Family vacations. Favorite Christmas gifts. Grandpa Holloway dancing at the family reunion. The time the bird flew into my plate of food on a camping trip. The stories Papa Perkins told. We have those memories in common.

In some ways, I'm not very close to my brothers. We don't get to spend much time with each other. In another way, we are as close as we can be. After all, we are brothers. We share a common father. It is our love for him and for mom that binds us together.

We share the same flesh and blood.

In the same way, it is God our Father and our common relationship with him that makes us one. You don't get to choose the Christians you unite with. God alone does that.

The second reaction I hear to Christian unity is, "Good luck with that. It will never happen." This answer confuses unity with human work. It assumes we can come up with a plan to unify Christians.

But Christian unity is the work of God. Working for unity is a matter of faith. We are taught to pray, "Your will be done on earth as it is in heaven." Yet if we watch or read the news, it does not look as if God's will is done here as it is in heaven. We don't see how it could be. But we walk by faith, not sight. We trust that God is working to bring in his will on our earth. In the same way, we pray and work for Christian unity, trusting that God will make it happen.

A third reaction I hear to Christian unity is, "Wouldn't that be nice." In other words, unity would be a good thing, but it's not really an important thing. Yet if one reads the Bible, one finds that unity lies at the very heart of God. Unity is the theme of the entire Bible. God created the world in love. He made humans so he could love them. But they turned against him and rejected his love. So God became human. "The Word became flesh and lived among us." He gave himself for humanity to reconcile them to himself. His desire is for all humans to be one with him and one with each other. Every story in the Bible, and our personal stories, is part of that big story of a God who wants unity.

Unity is more than a nice thing. It is a priority to God. It was so important to Jesus that he prayed for it while facing death.

So what is the proper response to Jesus' prayer for unity? It must be "Yes! Yes, Lord! Let it be! Bring it on!"

Act Locally

If that is our reaction, then how do we begin to work for Christian unity? I do not have the easy steps to unity. But I have a first step.

The step Jesus made. Facing the cross, Jesus did not give a plan for unity but he did offer a prayer for it. Our first step is to pray. Do you pray for the unity of all Christians? How often? Is it part of your daily prayer? Does your church pray for Christian unity? Since unity is God's work, we begin by humbly yet boldly asking for it.

But prayer is dangerous. If you pray for God to do something, he might do it through you! So as we pray for Christian unity, we develop a passion for Christian unity. Nothing is more important to God. It must become central in importance to us. And if we have that passion, then we must practice Christian unity.

That's why in the prayer of Jesus, Christian unity, as wonderful as it is, is not an end in itself. It is unity for the sake of the world. Unity and evangelism go hand in hand.

Why is our evangelism so ineffective at times? Perhaps because our neighbors cannot see the good news in Christians who are divided among themselves. Christian unity leads to effective evangelism. Our neighbors know the love of God when they see Christians loving one another and loving others.

Let us end where we began. My mother's last words to me, "Watch out for your brother." Our Savior's last words to us, "Watch out for your brother; watch out for your sister." That's what Christianity unity is all about.

DAY 26

Amazing Grace

Mark 15:1-39

Crosses. We see them every day. On churches and hospitals. In cemeteries. On tee-shirts and bumper stickers. Ballplayers make the sign of the cross before they step in to hit or after they score a touchdown.

Crosses have even become fashionable accessories, worn on necklaces and as earrings. Sometimes worn by people who have no Christian beliefs and even an anti-Christian lifestyle.

If you are a Christian, you not only see crosses in the world, but you probably have some in your home. We sing songs about the cross, hear sermons on the cross, and pledge to take up the cross. Many songs. Many sermons. many pledges.

When is the last time you cried over the cross?

The cross. We see it so frequently that all the meaning has been sucked from it.

We are no longer amazed by the cross.

Amazing Scandal

"Jews demand miraculous signs and Greeks look for wisdom, but we preach Christ crucified: a stumbling block to Jews and foolishness to Gentiles. . . ."

1 Corinthians 1:22-23

Unlike today, in the culture of the New Testament, the cross had meaning. But not the meaning we think it did.

The cross was not a positive symbol. It was as far as one could get from a religious symbol.

Cross mean crucifixion. Torture. Pain. Punishment. Shame.

It was extremely difficult to get people to follow a man who died on a cross. Why? Because the cross was a symbol of horror. Crucifixion was slow torture. Perhaps you've read articles or heard sermons that described in great detail the agonies of one on a cross. One who faced crucifixion was first beaten severely, until the skin was flayed, the blood flowed freely, and sometimes even the muscles and internal organs were exposed to view. Then one was forced to carry the heavy cross-bar to the place of execution. Then the real torture began. Hands and feet nailed. Hanging on the cross by those hands and feet for hours, sometimes for days. In agony. Unable to draw a deep breath. Watching one's life drip away slowly into the ground at your feet.

But the cross was not only painful, it was shameful. Crucifixion was saved only for the lowest of the low. Slaves, traitors, and rebels were put on crosses. It was not a death for respectable murderers. It was intended to add insult to injury. It was capital punishment for the worst of crimes.

Why would people be reluctant to follow one who was crucified? Because his shame would fall on them. Crucifixion was execution of a criminal. Can you imagine people today following a leader who was executed? Can you imagine them saying, "We follow the electrocuted one." Or "We glory in the gallows." Can you imagine buildings decorated with the hangman's noose or people wearing small silver replicas of a man in an electric chair? Yet that was the shame of the cross. Jesus died a failure and a criminal.

The cross meant pain and shame. It also meant guilt. Deuteronomy 21:23 says, "anyone hung on a tree is under God's curse." The Jews understood that to mean that God cursed anyone who was crucified.

No wonder the message of the cross was such a scandal to those who first heard it. To the Gentiles, the idea that the Son of God would die on the cross was foolishness (1 Corinthians 1:23). It was stupid. God cannot die! Much less can he die such a painful, humiliating death. To Jews, the idea of a crucified Messiah was unthinkable. The Messiah was to save others. He was to lead his people into his kingdom. He was to conquer the kingdoms of the earth, not die at their hand like a common criminal. A crucified Messiah was a contradiction in terms like "boiling ice" or "cold fire." The Messiah was to triumph, not to fail.

Amazed Disciples

"'The Son of Man is going to be betrayed into the hands of men. They will kill him, and after three days he will rise.' But they did not understand what he meant." Mark 9:31b–32a

One of the great mysteries to people who read the Gospels is the stupidity of the disciples. Why couldn't they see that Jesus came to die for our sins? Why didn't they expect the crucifixion? It's especially hard to understand their stupidity when Jesus tells them plainly that he will die and they *still* do not understand. Why couldn't they see what is so plain to us?

Because a crucified Messiah was unthinkable. That's why the disciples couldn't accept the idea.

Because they understood crucifixion and we do not. They knew its pain and shame and horror. They could not imagine that it was God's will to put Jesus through that.

But it was.

We have an advantage over the disciples. We know Jesus came to die for our sins. What we don't know (or perhaps do not want to know) is how unthinkable, how amazing, his death really is.

Or perhaps we do. Perhaps we are no different from the disciples. Perhaps, like them, we want a Jesus who is triumphant. We want a Jesus who helps us through our troubles, who improves our family life, who encourages us when we are down, who builds our self-esteem and helps us reach our full potential. Reigning at his right or left hand sounds too "pie in the sky" for us. We want happiness now and we believe Jesus will give it to us.

He won't.

"Wait a minute," you say. "Didn't Jesus promise that if we seek first his kingdom that all other things would be added to us (Matthew 6:33)? Didn't he promise abundant life (John 10:10)?"

Yes, but first he promised a cross. Like James and John, we must first be willing to drink the cup of Jesus and be baptized with his baptism. We must submit to death before life. And no ordinary death. Death on a cross. Crucifixion. Nails through flesh. Naked. Ashamed. Guilty. Only then can we know life. Cross always comes before crown. We know Jesus as executioner before we know him as friend. As Dietrich Bonhoeffer said, "The cross of Christ forever destroyed the equation 'religion equals happiness.'"

Is it any wonder that disciples then and now want to avoid the cross?

Are You Amazed?

"But God proves his love for us in that while we still were sinners Christ died for us." Romans 5:8 (NRSV)

Can we still be amazed by the cross? Or have there been too many church signs, too many necklaces and earrings, too many hymns, too many sermons?

Can we still be amazed at the depth of God's love? That he sent his Son. To die. On a cross. For us. While we were still sinners.

Are we amazed that the Son of God died for us? And that he died in this way. On a cross. Naked. Ashamed. Cursed. Alone.

And the most amazing thing of all. He died for me.

In the words of Charles H. Gabriel:

> I stand amazed in the presence of Jesus the Nazarene,
> and wonder how he could love me,
> a sinner, condemned, unclean.

We Stand Amazed

But are we amazed enough to do the most amazing thing of all? Are we amazed enough to follow Jesus? If so, how do we follow? "Then he said to them all: 'If anyone would come after me, he must deny himself and take up his cross daily and follow me. For whoever wants to save his life will lose it, but whoever loses his life for me will save it'" (Luke 9:23-24).

Are you amazed at the cross? Amazed enough to follow Jesus? If so, one question remains: Are you amazed enough to die?

If so, that death comes daily. It begins tomorrow. When we wake up in the morning our first thought becomes, "This is the day I die." I'm not going to think any more about my hopes and dreams and desires. I no longer live my life. I'm dead. I live for others. I live to serve. I'm willing to embrace the pain, the torture, the suffering, the shame. All for the one who did it for me.

But where's the good news in all this? Where is the gospel?

The great good news is this: If we die with him, we will live with him.

Forever.

With that in mind, not even death, not even the cross, seems so bad.

DAY 27

The Greatest Miracle of All

Matthew 27:31-54

Another Day, Another Drachma

"Then they led him away to crucify him." Matthew 27:31

He was back home in Italy, by the sea. The tang of the salt air filled his lungs as a smile spread over his face. "Surely this is paradise," he thought.

Suddenly the sea faded, replaced by the homely face of one of his men.

"Wake up, sir. The governor wants to see you."

For a moment he wasn't sure where he was. Then it hit him. The heat, the smell. He wasn't back home by the sea; he was in the stinking province of Palestine. Oh well, no one ever told him that soldiering would be easy. He's been in enough stink-holes in his long career to have learned that. It was time to earn his pay. Another day, another drachma.

Putting on his uniform, he rushed to the governor's palace. Pilate had a job for him all right, an execution, in fact, three. He'd been in charge of countless crucifixions before. It wasn't his favorite job, but it was routine.

Two of the prisoners were like all the ones before them. They'd repeatedly broken the Roman peace, robbing their fellow Jews in the guise of freedom fighters. Hah! As if anyone in this accursed country could lead a successful rebellion. The third prisoner was different. He was being put to death because of some disagreements he had with the Jewish leaders over their laws. The Jews had convinced Pilate that he was politically dangerous, so he ordered him crucified. Word was that this man Jesus had not even tried to defend himself at his trial. "What a loser," thought the centurion.

Until he saw him. There was something in his eyes and in the way he walked. This Jesus didn't have the look of a prisoner. But that would change. Pilate had ordered him flogged. No one could stand a flogging and still keep his dignity.

"Strip him and beat him," the centurion ordered. As the flogging began, he was distracted by preparations for the crucifixion. "Are the crosses ready?" he asked the private. "Corporal, make sure you have enough men for crowd control." As he gave his orders, something nagged at the back of his mind. It was the flogging. Something wasn't quite right.

Then it hit him. The silence. This Jew Jesus was taking his beating in silence. Not a word escaped his lips. In all his years he'd never witnessed anything like it. Maybe there was some truth to those rumors that Jesus possessed some special power.

His thoughts were interrupted by another soldier calling him away for some last minute preparations. When he returned, he found his troops having fun at the expense of the prisoner. They'd heard that his crime was claiming to be King of the Jews, so they put a kingly robe on him, gave him a crown of thorns, and beat him on the head with his own wooden "scepter." While some spat at him, others kneeled before him. "Look at me guys," one said, "I'm joining with this Jewish king."

His first impulse was to break things up. Flogging and crucifixion were cruel enough without adding insult to injury. What stopped him in his tracks was the face of this Jesus. The insults fazed him not in the least. He sat there quietly as if nothing was happening. The centurion was shocked, and by the time he recovered, the soldiers were through with their fun.

They forced Jesus and the other prisoners to carry their crosses to Skull hill outside the city. Jesus fell repeatedly, until finally the centurion ran out of patience and grabbed someone from the crowd to carry his cross. As the procession wound through the city, the crowds jeered the prisoners, saving their most hateful threats for Jesus.

When they got to the Skull, the centurion was busy. He made sure the prisoners were nailed tight to their crosses and that they were raised in the proper manner. He had their charges nailed over them, including Jesus' crime: "King of the Jews." He let the soldiers gamble for the prisoners' clothes. Then, as he had done so many times before, he settled down to wait for them to die.

Something was different about this time. It all had to do with this prisoner Jesus. Something about his eyes. In pain, they still reflected his care for others. The crowd jeered at him. Even his fellow prisoners joined in. It didn't bother him. Indeed, his calmness caused one of the thieves to change his mind. This Jesus just didn't die like all the others.

Then the centurion heard the last words he ever expected to hear from one on a cross: "Father, forgive them, they do not know what they were doing." He'd been cursed so many times from so many crosses, that he paid no attention to it anymore. But he'd never been blessed, never forgiven. This Jesus was no ordinary man.

For hours the centurion stood there and watched him, transfixed by the way this Jesus died. Then he heard him cry in a loud voice. He couldn't understand the words, but he knew he was crying to his God.

Then Jesus died.

At that moment the centurion was startled. A strange darkness had covered the land for hours. Now the ground began to shake. He couldn't keep his footing. His men were terrified.

This hardened soldier, not prone to emotional outbursts, could not believe what he had witnessed. "Surely this was no ordinary man," he thought. "Surely he was innocent." "Surely, he was the Son of God."

Great Miracles

Here stands a pagan. An unbeliever. A hard-headed soldier not given to foolishness. He knew little of Jesus. He only knew how he died. But he is convinced. This Jesus is from God. It's not clear exactly what he confessed. According to Luke, he proclaimed Christ "righteous" or "innocent." Mark and Matthew say he called him "the Son of God," or, as some translations say, "a son of God." Whatever the depth of his confession, the amazing thing is that he had faith at all. He didn't see Jesus teaching the crowds. He didn't see him confound the religious teachers. He never saw him heal the sick or raise the dead. He wasn't at the empty tomb. He only saw him on the cross. That was enough.

What does it take for us to follow Jesus, to confess him each day as the Son of God? Does it take teaching that touches our hearts? Blessings? Miracles? Or like this centurion can we see him at his greatest defeat, at the lowest point of his life, and still see there the Holy Son of God? We see him at the cross. He bids us to take our own and follow.

Is the crucifixion a miracle? Certainly miracles surround it: darkness, earthquake, even dead brought back to life (Matthew 27:52-53). When Jesus dies, another miracle takes place that we are prone to overlook: "At that moment the curtain of the temple was torn in two from top to bottom" (Matthew 27:51).

There is something in these few words that strikes at the heart of what it means to be a Christian. We all know the significance of the tearing of the temple curtain or veil. This was the thick curtain that divided the Holy Place from the Most Holy Place. The Presence of God inhabited the Most Holy Place in some special way. It was so holy, that only the high priest could enter, then only once a year on the day of atonement, and only with sacrificial blood for his own sins.

The symbolism of the torn curtain is clear: through Jesus' death, the path to God is opened to everyone. All may approach God's holy throne through the blood of Jesus. We no longer need a human priest to stand between us and God. Christ alone is our mediator and we all are priests. God himself will now hear our requests through Jesus Christ.

But the part of the verse we may miss is that the curtain is torn *from top to bottom*. In other words, it was no human act that opened the way to God. It was no super-human effort on our part that scaled the heights to bring God down to us. No! It was God and God alone in the person of his Son who opens the door for us.

This is not just a story about how a curtain was torn, it is a metaphor for the whole of the Christian life. Too many times we live as if the depth of our relationship to God was all up to us. If only we could sin less and pray more. If only we had the right technique, the right steps. If only we could find the right book that would unlock the secret of spirituality.

It doesn't work that way. Christian faith and spirituality don't come from the bottom up. They come from the top down. God does them for us. He opens the way. Yes, we must walk through the curtain, but even there we have someone to follow. We follow in the steps of One whose love and obedience and very blood opened the curtain for us. He ripped it open, from top to bottom.

Jesus' death on the cross is a deed of power. It is also a wonder. A wonder is something that astonishes and surprises. Something uncanny, almost terrifying.

Here is the greatest wonder of all: not how he died, but why he died. He died for me, for you. Such love shocks us. We gaze open-mouthed at this one on the cross. He is a wonder. The greatest wonder of them all. The greatest miracle.

Power. Wonder. Miracles are also signs. A sign points to something beyond itself. The miracles of Jesus point to a deeper reality. They point to God. The cross is a signpost of the love of God. In the cross we clearly see the God of love. He loved us so much he sent his Son to die for us. We did not, we do not deserve such love. Still he loves, for his love is free. Free to us. Costly to him. In the cross we see a sign of that awful cost. Here the Son of God, God himself, pays the ultimate price of love.

We are all familiar with signs of love. We see then daily. A guy gives a girl his class ring. A little girl writes her mother a sweet note. A grandfather passes on a cherished book to his grandson. We treasure the ring, the note, the book, not because they are valuable in themselves, but because they are signs of love.

Here is a miracle we see each day. The miracle that God loved us and sent his Son. The miracle that Jesus died for sinners. The miracle that his death continues to cleanse us from sin. Through him we perform a miracle, the miracle of discipleship. By his power we die each day. We take the cross. Each day we gaze at the cross as this centurion did and we confess what he confessed: "Surely this was, surely this is, the Son of God."

The greatest miracle of all.

DAY 28

An Unexpected Return

Luke 24:13-35

"Were not our hearts burning within us. . . ?" Luke 24:32a

No one expected the resurrection.

Jesus clearly predicted his resurrection, but when it happened no one expected it. The women came to the tomb to anoint a dead body, not to greet a risen Lord. They worried over how they would roll away the stone; they didn't know it was already removed. Even after seeing the empty tomb and hearing the news of the resurrection from the young man in the white robe, they flee in tomb in fright, "trembling and bewildered" (Mark 16:8).

No one expected his appearances. The two on the road to Emmaus at first don't even recognize the risen Lord. The apostles are cowering in fear even *after* they hear of the resurrection. When he appears, it always startles, always catches them off guard. The Jesus who was a constant surprise during his life continues to shock after his death and resurrection.

We may marvel at the slowness of the disciples. If Jesus said he would rise again (and he did), why didn't they expect it? Why was it so hard to believe? How could they be so hard-hearted and hard-headed?

We'd better not be too tough on these early disciples. We might find the stones we throw rebounding in our own direction. Jesus clearly predicted his death and resurrection. Just as clearly he predicted his return at the end of the age. They were caught off guard by the empty tomb and the risen Lord. We must not be caught off guard by the last trumpet and the returning Lord. As we look again at the startled faces of the disciples who saw their crucified Lord alive, let us resolve to live in expectation of the time when every eye will see him. That great miracle is still to come.

Heartburn

It was a strange and perilous journey. It began with two friends, setting out for Jerusalem for the feast of Passover. They had made the journey together before; it had been neither strange nor perilous.

But this time it was different. This time things happened in Jerusalem that had never happened before. Strange things that would change their lives.

It began the day they arrived. Coming into the city they noticed a commotion. A crowd was rushing out the gate. "What's happening?" they wondered, and finally got the courage to ask a passing woman.

"It's Jesus from Nazareth," she breathlessly replied, "He's coming into the city, riding a donkey like a king."

"What do you mean, 'Like a king?'" But she had already rushed away.

Deciding to see for themselves, they pushed through the crowd to the roadside. Many had stripped the nearby palm trees for their branches.

And then he came.

He looked in many ways like any other man. And yet there was something about him, a presence, an authority. As he got closer, the crowd went wild, placing palm branches in his path and calling him the Son of David.

"Who is this Jesus?" they wondered.

In the days to come they were to find out. They watched open-mouthed as he overturned the moneychangers' tables in the temple. They witnessed his contests of wits with the scribes and Pharisees. They even visited with his disciples and learned of his miracles, of his teaching, and of his kingdom. Finally they were convinced. In this, the strangest week of their lives, they had come to believe that this rabbi from Nazareth was the one they had sought. He was the Savior, the Messiah.

They were there when he was killed.

Having placed all their hopes on him, they saw their hopes die with him, locked away forever in a garden tomb.

But then came the strangest part of all. Some of the women disciples told them they had found the tomb empty and that angels had appeared and told them Jesus was alive.

The two friends didn't believe them. Having made the perilous journey to faith only to have that faith crushed, they were not about to believe such a story. Jesus may have had the power to heal and even to raise others from the dead, but it was too much to believe that he was alive again. They had watched him die.

So they started home.

They walked in silence for a while, then began to discuss this week that had turned them inside out. They were overtaken by a stranger. He was going their way and asked if he could tag along. "Sure," they said.

"I couldn't help but notice you were deep in conversation when I interrupted you. What were you talking about?"

"Oh, about this past week in Jerusalem."

"What about it?"

"Oh, you know, about Jesus of Nazareth."

"What about him?"

"You've come from Jerusalem and don't know about Jesus?"

So they told the stranger of their incredible week, how they had pinned all their hopes on this Jesus, but how it had all come to nothing. He had been killed.

"But wasn't the Messiah supposed to be killed?" he said. And he began to give them the most marvelous Bible lesson they had ever heard, quoting scriptures from Moses to the prophets.

Soon it was supper time and they invited the stranger to eat with them at a local inn. At first he said no, but they finally convinced him. At the meal, he took the bread, blessed it, broke it, and gave it to them.

And then it happened. Suddenly they saw him clearly. It was Jesus! Alive! Their hope was not in vain.

As soon as they recognized him, he disappeared. Leaving supper on the table, they hurried back to Jerusalem to tell his disciples.

"We should have known sooner," they said, "For while he talked with us on the road, our hearts burned within us."

How can we be sure Jesus is the Son of God? One can give many logical proofs, can make many good arguments, but how can we know?

We know because our hearts burn within us. By faith we have seen Jesus, we have heard his voice along the roads of our own lives. We have recognized him at his table when the bread is broken. At times we may be blind. Like these two friends, we do not recognize him. But even in those times of doubt, our eyes are opened. Looking back, we too can only wonder how we failed to see him. For his words burn deep into our hearts.

Locked Doors

They'd just gotten the news.

Mary of Magdala had returned from the tomb and announced, "I have seen the Lord!" (John 20:18). Breathlessly she told them of her early morning visit. She had found the tomb empty and had run to Peter and John in distress. "Someone's taken the Lord's body and we don't know where it is!" Peter and John ran to the tomb and found it as she described. It was empty. They returned to their homes wondering what it meant.

But Mary had returned to the tomb, distraught. Crying bitterly, she wondered, "Why can't they just leave him alone? They've even taken his body before we can give it a proper anointing." She wept from sorrow and anger. She decided to look in the tomb one more time. Maybe she'd just imagined it. Maybe he was really there.

And there was someone there! Two someones dressed in white. "Why are you crying?" they asked.

"They have taken my Lord away and I don't know where they put him."

Suddenly she noticed someone behind her. "Who are you looking for?" he asked.

"Finally," she thought, "here's someone who can help." She thought he was the caretaker. If anyone knew what had happened to Jesus' body, it was he. "If you put his body somewhere, just tell me where he is and I'll get him," she cried.

"Mary," he said.

And in that one word she recognized him.

In joy she held him until he had to tell her to let go. "Tell the others," he said.

So she did. She ran and told the disciples who were meeting in the upper room.

They met at night. In secret. Behind locked doors. Afraid of the Jewish authorities. After all, they'd seen what had happened to Jesus. None of them wanted to be crucified.

One would think that Mary's news would have changed all that. If Jesus is risen, then whom should they fear? Perhaps it was their lack of faith, perhaps cowardice, perhaps an understandable caution. For whatever reason, the doors were locked.

Suddenly Jesus stood among them. He was no ghost! They saw his wounded hands and side. They were beside themselves with joy. The Lord is alive! Jesus even breathes the Holy Spirit upon them. Then he disappears.

Now they had seen him themselves. Now the Spirit was upon them. Now we expect them to have faith and courage. But one was not there. Thomas refuses to believe unless he can put his own hands in the wounds of Jesus. So a week later they are in the house again.

The doors were locked.

Why? Were they still afraid? It appears so. Thomas is the one called "doubting," but in spite of what they had seen and what had been given to them, the other disciples lock the door. What were they afraid of? If God can raise Jesus from the dead, what enemy can overcome them? What's the worst thing that could happen to them? Torture? Death? Jesus endured both and now stands before them a second time. Alive!

Being an eyewitness of the resurrection didn't keep them from fear. The Holy Spirit did not give them the confidence to leave the doors unlocked. We marvel at their lack of trust. Have we more faith than they?

Thomas sees and believes. Jesus says, "Because you have seen me, you have believed; blessed are those who have not seen and yet have believed" (John 20:29). Do you believe in the resurrection? Then

Christ blesses you. Do you believe in the resurrection? Then why do you fear? Why lock your doors?

There's nothing wrong with locking the doors to our cars, our homes, our offices. It is prudent to do so. But how many of us claim to be Christians, believers in a risen Lord, and continue to live our lives in fear? We lock the doors of our hearts to anyone and anything that might threaten. We put our trust in safety and precautions, not in the God who raised Jesus from the dead.

What's the worst that can happen to us? We'll be hurt. Abused. Taken advantage of. Cheated. Unjustly imprisoned. Beaten. Killed. Or perhaps the worst that will happen is we'll live our lives feeling unfulfilled, unappreciated, facing mid-life crises and a slow end in a nursing home. God delivered Jesus from death. Can he not deliver us from whatever it is we fear?

He will. He does. And we dare not live our lives like these fearful disciples. We believe in this great miracle of resurrection. He lives! He lives for us. We live now and will live again through him.

He stands at the door and knocks.

Unlock the door.

Let him in.

DAY 29

Where Is Jesus?

Luke 24:50-53; Acts 1:1-11

Where is Jesus? It's a serious question, not like "Where's Waldo?"

If you ask children in a Sunday school class, they are likely to give you one of three answers (with appropriate gestures).

"He's in heaven" (finger pointed upward).

"He's everywhere" (with arms waving).

"He's in here" (with finger pointed toward their hearts).

It's the same answer (perhaps without the gestures) you would get from adults.

Jesus Is in Heaven

Christians rightly focus on the stories of the crucifixion and resurrection, but there's another important part of the story that follows. The ascension. It's a story that answers the question, "Where is Jesus?"

Luke tells the story in two parts, one in his Gospel and one in Acts. For Luke, the ascension is the hinge pin of the two volumes he writes about Jesus.

> When he had led them out to the vicinity of Bethany, he lifted up his hands and blessed them. While he was blessing them, he left them and was taken up into heaven. Then they worshiped him and returned to Jerusalem with great joy. And they stayed continually at the temple, praising God.
> Luke 24:50-53

> After he said this, he was taken up before their very eyes, and a cloud hid him from their sight.
>
> They were looking intently up into the sky as he was going, when suddenly two men dressed in white stood beside them. "Men of Galilee," they said, "why do you stand here looking into the sky? This same Jesus, who has been taken from you into heaven, will come back in the same way you have seen him go into heaven." Acts 1:9-11

Where is Jesus? He has gone into the sky, taken up to heaven. But where is heaven? Is it literally up? Just above the clouds? But we've flown up there and not seen it. Perhaps it is farther up. If we had a powerful spaceship could we get there.

We know better. Heaven is not a place to get to in a spaceship. Heaven is a real place but a spiritual place. In short, heaven is where God lives.

But isn't God everywhere? What do we mean God lives in heaven? What do we mean that Jesus is in heaven? What is heaven? Where is heaven?

It is understandable that children would think of heaven in spatial terms. Heaven is up. But more mature Christians should think in more spiritual terms. Heaven is that place where the presence of God is immediate. We see him face to face. Heaven is where God's will is done completely. Heaven is filled with God's glorious presence.

This is why the Bible seldom talks of "going to heaven" but rather of heaven coming to us. Jesus will return and bring with him a new heaven and new earth, an earth where he reigns completely. When we say Jesus is in heaven, we mean he enjoys the glory he has as the Son of God.

Jesus Is Here

But Jesus did not ascend to leave us alone. He does not say to us as his disciples, "I've done my work. You are on your own now. Do the best you can."

On the contrary, he assures his disciples that he (in one sense) is not leaving them. He is leaving only so he can be with us in a deeper way. Not just with us in the flesh, but in our bodies. For we are the body of Christ. Jesus says it is better for us that he leaves. Only then can he send his Spirit to be in us.

> Now I am going to him who sent me, yet none of you asks me, 'Where are you going?' Because I have said these things, you are filled with grief. But I tell you the truth: It is for your good that I am going away. Unless I go away, the Counselor will not come to you; but if I go, I will send him to you. John 16:5-7

We sometimes envy the first disciples because they saw Jesus in the flesh. But we have a deeper presence of Jesus. He lives in us through his Holy Spirit! The ascension therefore is not a story of absence but one of presence. While he was here in a physical body Jesus had the limitations all humans have. He could only be one place at a time. He could only be with a limited number of people at a time. By ascending to the Father, he now can be in anyone anywhere through his Holy Spirit. Jesus did not leave! He lives in us!

Celebrating the Ascension

Think of what Jesus has done for us. He became one of us, taking on the limits and pains of being human. He taught us by embodying the truth of God. He submitted his will to the Father and went to the cross for us. He was raised so that we might be raised with him.

Then he left.

But he left for us. He left, not to be apart from us, but to be with us in the most intimate way. He now lives, not with us, but in us. "On that day you will realize that I am in my Father, and you are in me, and I am in you."

Do we realize it? If so, as we rightly celebrate the death and resurrection of Christ, let us likewise celebrate his ascension. He ascends to give us the greatest gift of all, his Holy Spirit presence. Jesus is in heaven. Jesus is in us. Jesus is present in the world through his Spirit.

DAY 30

A Church of Signs and Wonders

Acts 2:43-47

"Many wonders and miraculous signs were done by the apostles." Acts 2:43b

Imagine. Imagine we are sitting here and suddenly we hear a sound like a hurricane. The room trembles and we fear the walls and roof will collapse.

Now imagine looking at the person beside you. On his head is a flame. His head does not burn, but you see the flame. What would you think?

Then you hear the person on the other side of you speak. She speaks in a language you have never heard before, yet you know it is a language.

Imagine. How would you feel if you witnessed all these things?

If you know your Bible, you know there were some who did not have to imagine. On Pentecost after the resurrection of Jesus, the sound of a tornado fills the room, tongues of fire appear, the Holy

Spirit fills some of the disciples, and they speak in other tongues. What happens in that upper room spills into the city streets. People begin to ask, what does this mean—wind, fire, and languages?

How exciting to be at Pentecost. But the highpoint of the day, the greatest miracle, is not wind or fire or tongues. It is a sermon.

Are you disappointed? If your neighbor asks, "What did you do yesterday?" and you can answer, "I heard a wind, saw flames of fire, and heard people speak languages they did not learn," then your neighbor would be impressed. How exciting! But if you say, "I heard a sermon," you likely would not receive an excited response from your neighbor.

But on that day of Pentecost, the highpoint was a sermon. For it was not the wind, fire, and tongues that were so amazing. It was Peter's explanation of them. Peter tells the crowd of Jesus, one "accredited by God to you by miracles, wonders, and signs" (Acts 2:22). Peter calls them to faith in Jesus. Three thousand respond and are baptized. The church begins with miracles.

We envy those eyewitnesses of Jesus. We envy the apostles who worked wonders and signs. We have no apostles around today. We may not see the blind healed or the dead raised with our own eyes.

Or do we? I have never seen one born blind receive his sight. I've never seen one raised from the dead. I have seen Jesus work in my life and in the lives of those around me. I've prayed for the sick. He healed them. I've begged for forgiveness. He cleansed me. I've asked for wisdom. He guided me. He works in amazing ways, miraculous ways. He still works wonders.

The proper response to miracle is devotion. Miracles caused excitement and enthusiasm. The Spirit transformed that momentary enthusiasm into permanent devotion. To be devoted to something means to make it a constant practice. It implies dedication, discipline, and habit. The Jerusalem Christians experienced the thrill of miracle, but they wanted more. From them we learn to devote ourselves to a life of discipleship. A life of more.

Learn More

"They devoted themselves to the apostles' teaching. . . ." Acts 2:42a

These first believers had come to Jerusalem from all over the world to celebrate Pentecost. While there they found their lives radically changed. Now they believed that Jesus was the promised Messiah they had awaited.

But what did they know of Jesus? Some perhaps had seen his miracles and heard his teaching. Others knew very little. They might not have known that Jesus healed the lame, cast out demons, and raised the dead. They may not have heard that he taught, "Love your enemies." They had been baptized in his name. They had dedicated their whole lives to him. They wanted to know more of this Messiah who saved them.

Who's going to teach them? Who better than the apostles? They had been with Jesus. They had seen his signs and heard his teaching. They were witnesses to his resurrection. No wonder these early Christians wanted to sit at their feet and learn of the Savior.

By faith we see the miracles of Jesus. We hear his teaching. If we want to know more, we go to the same source as these first believers. We go to the teachings of the disciples about Jesus. We read those teachings in the Gospels, and the more we read and reflect and pray, the more we want to know about our Savior.

Are we devoted to the apostles' teaching? Do we want to know more of Jesus? Of course. By looking at his miracles, we are moved to dedicate ourselves to study so we may know him more.

Share More

These first believers were dedicated to fellowship. Many of us can't separate the word "fellowship" from eating. It conjures up memories of church suppers, potlucks, and dinners on the ground. These Pentecost believers also ate together from house to house. Three thousand converts at Pentecost. Many of them must have been strangers to each other. How do you get to know someone? By sharing a meal. By "doing lunch." We still do it that way today.

But fellowship is more than eating together. The Greek word here is one of the few that most Christians know, *koinonia*. It is best translated "sharing." These Christians shared their food, but they shared much more. They even shared their money. "Selling their possessions and goods, they gave to everyone as he had need" (Acts 2:45). Here is the true test of Christian fellowship: Are you willing to cash in your investments to help a Christian brother or sister? These early disciples, though strangers to each other, were willing even to share their goods.

Most importantly, they shared their faith. This is what they had in common: they all had come to faith in Jesus. So they shared their food, their possessions, their inmost thoughts, their very lives. What brought them together was not what they had in common. What brought them together was the miraculous power of Jesus. Because they wanted to know him more, they also wanted to share with each other more.

Pray More

These converts were all Jews. They knew how to pray. They still needed to learn to pray as Jesus prayed. Many of them knew little of Jesus' teachings on prayer. Imagine hearing the Lord's Prayer for the first time. Imagine their surprise when they heard they must pray even for their enemies. These converts learned to pray from Jesus by way of the apostles. They learned to devote themselves to prayer.

The apostles were more than teachers of prayer. They practiced what they preached. A dispute arose in the church concerning the distribution of food to widows. The church appointed seven men to feed the widows so the apostles could "devote themselves to prayer and to serving the word" (Acts 6:4). Fellowship, that is, sharing with the poor, is certainly an act close to the heart of God. So is prayer. The early church neglected neither. Like Jesus before them they developed a habit of prayer.

What power these early Christians had! What fellowship! What was their secret? The miraculous power of Jesus? Of course. Their experience of the Spirit? Certainly. But they also knew the secret of prayer. The early church was a praying church. That was the source of their power. If we are to recapture their faith and their witness, we must learn to be devoted to prayer. We want to pray more to a powerful Father. We want to pray more with a loving Savior. We want to pray more in the power of the Spirit.

Worship More

The early church met to worship God in the name of the Lord Jesus. The wonders and miracles of Jesus and the apostles were signs. They pointed to the love and power of the heavenly Father. At the miraculous catch of fish, Peter faced that holy power and love in the person of Jesus. He responded in fear, falling at Jesus feet and saying, "Depart from me for I am sinful man" (Luke 5:8). Thomas faced that holy power in the resurrected Jesus and worshipped, saying, "My Lord and my God!" (John 20:28).

These believers saw the power of God in the miracles of Pentecost. They react with fear. "Everyone was filled with awe. . ." (Acts 2:43). Holy fear is the ground of worship. "But why should we fear God?" you ask. "Isn't he a loving Father?" Yes. Oh, yes. But he is also the Almighty. He is an awesome God. "Awesome" has lost much of its original punch. Today we call everything from the latest fashions to the newest car "awesome." Perhaps some older translations are closer to the mark when they call God an "awful" God. He is not awful in the contemporary sense of the word, but he is one who inspires fear, awe, and reverence.

When we see the power of God in the miracles of Jesus we are awestruck. They bring us to our knees in worship. We bow before a God whose holiness and power scare us.

How do we express that reverent fear? These early Christians expressed it in the breaking of the bread. As we saw above, this phrase refers to eating together with fellow Christians. It also refers to eating with Jesus. At the Lord's Supper we come in contact with the Holy One of Israel. To the early church, the Lord's Meal was so central to their worship that their entire purpose for meeting is summed up in the phrase, "we came together to break bread" (Acts 20:7).

Each Sunday we witness a miracle. Jesus comes and eats with us! We share a meal with the one who stilled the waves, multiplied the loaves, and even defeated death. How can we approach this meal except with awe? How can we leave without wanting to worship him more?

Rejoice More

The Jerusalem church had "glad and sincere hearts" (Acts 2:46). They were happy people, but they had more than their share of trouble. Christian happiness is not based on circumstances. It is a miracle. Christ alone makes our hearts glad. These early Christians would soon know persecution. Some, like the apostles, would be beaten and thrown in jail. Some, like Stephen, would even give their lives for the faith. No matter. They still were happy. After the apostles are flogged by the Sanhedrin, they leave "rejoicing because they had been counted worthy of suffering disgrace for the Name" (Acts 5:41).

How do we react when we see the miracles of Jesus? We rejoice. We dedicate ourselves to him even if it means suffering. If hard times come because of Jesus, our hearts are still glad. We suffer because he suffered for us. Here is happiness the world can never understand, not the shallow happiness that all experience when things are going great. No, this is the deep and powerful joy that comes when the wonderful power of Jesus lives in us. He died for us. We died with him. He was raised for us. We were raised with him. He gives us the miracle of new hearts. Hearts of gladness and joy.

Grow More

We hear much today about church growth. Every year it seems a new technique comes along as a sure-fire way to make new converts. All Christians want the church to grow because, like God himself, we want all people to be saved. We have seen the signs of Jesus in our lives, so we want others to experience his saving power.

Yet we struggle with the how. How do we take the gospel to our neighbors? How can we let them know the joy we feel? How can we reach those who know about Jesus, but don't really know him? Like the Pharisees, they see his miraculous works, but can't see who he is. How do we help the church grow?

The early Jerusalem church was a growing church. It begins with three thousand. Soon afterward their number grows to five thousand (Acts 4:4). Eventually they must have given up counting, for Luke simply says, "The number of disciples in Jerusalem increased rapidly" (Acts 6:7).

How do we explain this rapid growth? Did these Christians evangelize? I'm sure they did. They overcame their fear to tell their neighbors the good news of Jesus. Did they grow because of the wonders done by the apostles? No doubt those miracles convinced many. But what was their real secret of church growth?

Their secret was this: They were devoted to Jesus, not to growth. As Luke puts it: "And the Lord added to their number daily those who were being saved" (Acts 2:47).

The Lord added. It's not our church. It's the Lord's church. Church growth is not our job. It's his. He alone works the miracle of salvation in the hearts of human beings. Our part is to witness to what he has done for us. We tell others of his wonders. He works the wonder in them. His power is not limited by how well we tell the story or what techniques we use to motivate others to believe. Like the apostles, we are to tell the story of Jesus. The old, old story. We tell it clearly. We tell it boldly. But the power is in the story, not in our telling. The power, the sign, the wonder of Jesus and his love.

Complacency, Excitement, or Devotion?

When we look at the miracles we have a choice. We can react with complacency. Even boredom. We've heard all this before. It is an old, old story to many of us. We can look at the miracles of Jesus and feel nothing.

Or we can see them through fresh eyes. Like the blind man, we can feel the touch of Jesus and see what we could not see before. We can catch some of the excitement the original witnesses felt as they saw these amazing acts. What is more, we feel the excitement of knowing Jesus still works in our lives today. We may not understand why or how, but we know he is there for us.

That excitement might last for moments, perhaps even for days. It will not last forever. It must be turned into something permanent. In Jesus' day, there were those who witnessed the miracles, who were amazed, who were excited, but they never became disciples. The miracles are there to give us faith. Faith in the one who still works wonders. It is a faith that wants more. A faith that is devoted, no matter what the cost. We want, not the sign, but the one the sign points to.

We want not a wonder, but one named Wonderful. We want the greatest miracle of all.

A miracle named Jesus.

DAY 31

An Uncanny Resemblance

1 John 1:3

Now that we've seen the surprising Jesus, what are we going to do with him? Or (more importantly), what is he going to do with us? Like the first disciples, we don't always understand him. Even when we do, if we're honest we'll have to admit we don't always like what he says. "Go, sell all you have and give to the poor and come follow me." "Take up your cross daily." "The greatest is one who serves." Are we really thrilled by such teaching?

So, like the first disciples, we have to admit in our saner moments that we don't know how to follow this unexpected Jesus. We're not sure how to love him. Even when we are, we sometimes cannot bring ourselves to.

So what can we do? Nothing. We are saved by amazing grace. We just follow as best we can. And as we follow in our own feeble way, we begin to find a strange thing happening. Through the power of God we grow closer to this strange, demanding Lord and closer to each other. One of the greatest expressions of that closeness is found, not in the Gospels, but in the first letter of John.

Fellowship

"And our fellowship is with the Father and with his Son, Jesus Christ."

1 John 1:3b

Fellowship. In Bible times it was more than a church word. It had its background in the business world. If two people owned a business together, they had fellowship. Thus fellowship is partnership, joint participation, and co-ownership. This type of partnership is not easily broken. If you've ever gone into business with someone, you know it takes trust. You place your financial survival in your partners' hands. You not only need faith that he won't run off with the payroll, but also trust that he will give full effort to the business as you do. "Fellowship" thus entails trust, responsibility, and sharing of time and money.

Later the word grew beyond its business meaning to describe any kind of intimate relationship. A group who came together for the common good. A community that pulls together in crisis. A marriage. A family. All have fellowship, partnership, sharing, communion. In fellowship we become one with each other, we live in each other, we come to share a family resemblance.

Spitting Image

"Therefore be imitators of God, as beloved children. . . ." Ephesians 5:1 (NRSV)

A few years ago I received a small package from my aunt. Inside was an old family photograph of me and my cousins. I was in front with a little girl on my knee, my cousin Greg was standing behind me, my other cousins on either side. Suddenly it hit me. Something was wrong with the picture. Then "boom," it all came into focus. I wasn't in the picture at all; it was my father! It wasn't Greg, it was my uncle Leon. They weren't my cousins, but my uncles and aunts. I never thought I resembled dad very much, but in this picture I was his spitting image.

"She's the spitting image of her mother." You've said it. You've experienced it. That's the essence of fellowship: We become so like one another it's as if we shared DNA. We begin to look like them. The amazing message of 1 John is that our fellowship is with the Father and his Son, Jesus Christ. We are partners with God and Christ. They work with us, they work in us. But we are more than partners. We share so intimately in God and Christ that the Father even calls us his children: "How great is the love the Father has lavished on us, that we should be called children of God! And that is what we are!" (1 John 3:1). What greater fellowship, what greater intimacy can there be?

And as intimates of God, as children of God, we have a family resemblance to him. As we say in the South, we begin to "favor" God. We are being so conformed to Christ, so in fellowship with him, that we are becoming his spitting image. As Paul reminds us: "And we, who with unveiled faces all reflect the Lord's glory, are being transformed into his likeness with ever-increasing glory, which comes from the Lord, who is the Spirit" (2 Corinthians 3:18).

We are becoming like God. We begin to resemble Christ. This is the unbelievable message John has for us. Unbelievable because we know ourselves. We know the selfishness that still lurks in our hearts. We know the sins we can't quite seem to overcome. We know those closest to us whom we have hurt and neglected. It may be easy for us to believe we resemble the devil, but God? No way!

The Bible tells us otherwise. Whether we feel like it or not, we are God's children. As his children we have fellowship with him and Jesus. We bear his image. Each day we become more like him. Not because of our own innate goodness, but because God has given us his Spirit. Our fellowship comes from the Lord, from the Spirit who lives in us and is molding us into his likeness and glory.

And as we become more like him, we become more intimate with each other. The fellowship we have with fellow Christians flows directly from our fellowship with Christ. We are intimate with them because we have family ties: We share the same Father. Church is not an option, but a partnership: we share in Christ.

Resembling the Real Jesus

John begins his letter with a beautiful portrait of the One whom we resemble, the One who intimately shares with us:

> That which was from the beginning, which we have heard, which we have seen with our eyes, which we have looked at and our hands have touched-this we proclaim concerning the Word of life. The life appeared; we have seen it and testify to it, and we proclaim to you the eternal life, which was with the Father and has appeared to us. We proclaim to you what we have seen and heard, so that you also may have fellowship with us. And our fellowship is with the Father and with his Son, Jesus Christ. We write this to make our joy complete. 1 John 1:1-4

Like Genesis and the Gospel of John, 1 John begins with a bang, the big bang of creation. We have fellowship with the very One who made the universe. Before there was anything, he was there loving, planning, sharing with the Father and the Spirit. He was there to give shape to all that exists: "Through him all things were made; without him nothing was made that has been made" (John 1:3).

And we resemble the One who made all things! We share in the work of creation through Jesus. We show this family resemblance by exercising the creativity he has given us. In him, there is a new creation. We share in that creative act by proclaiming the message of reconciliation. (2 Corinthians 5:17-19). Those around us stare at the same old world and despair. We bring them the good news that a new world has come through Christ.

The heart of that good news of new creation is that the One from the beginning became flesh. God himself lived among us in the person of Jesus. John's fellowship with God was not just a way of thinking. It was more than a feeling. He heard God, saw him with his own eyes, even touched God in the person of Jesus. The Word of life was no mere message, it was flesh and blood.

How real is Jesus to you? As real as your husband, your wife, your parents, your children? As real as this page? As real as yourself? Do you hear him, see him, touch him each day? It is this real Jesus that John testifies to and proclaims. It is flesh and blood we meet in Scripture.

How do we feel when the flesh and blood Jesus lives in us? Joyous! John says "we write to make our joy complete." There is no greater joy in earth or heaven than to share with others in Christ. No greater joy than to testify and proclaim the Word of life. Why are we sometimes so joyless as Christians? Perhaps because we do not testify and proclaim. Who have you told about Jesus lately? Why haven't you told? Are you afraid you'll be embarrassed? You'll lose a friend? You'll look like a jerk? You know what will happen if you tell?

Joy. Pure joy.

So this book ends with an invitation. Through the eyes of the Gospel writers you've seen the flesh and blood Jesus. The shocking, surprising Jesus. The Jesus who calls you to leave all and follow him. To take up your cross.

If you hear and follow, you will find him not less, but even more surprising. We do not know where he will lead. But we do know if we follow him, no matter how much we stumble and fall, he is always there to lead us to life and joy and peace.

And as we follow, the most surprising thing of all: We begin to look like him.